Transmedia Theatre Plays

Transmedia Theatre Plays

A Contemporary Anthology

Edited by
CARIDAD SVICH

methuen | drama
LONDON • NEW YORK • OXFORD • NEW DELHI • SYDNEY

METHUEN DRAMA
Bloomsbury Publishing Plc, 50 Bedford Square, London, WC1B 3DP, UK
Bloomsbury Publishing Inc, 1385 Broadway, New York, NY 10018, USA
Bloomsbury Publishing Ireland, 29 Earlsfort Terrace, Dublin 2, D02 AY28, Ireland

BLOOMSBURY, METHUEN DRAMA and the Methuen Drama logo are trademarks of
Bloomsbury Publishing Plc

First published in Great Britain 2025

Copyright © Caridad Svich, 2025

The authors have asserted their right under the Copyright, Designs and Patents Act, 1988,
to be identified as authors of this work.

Cover design: Matt Thame

All rights reserved. No part of this publication may be: i) reproduced or transmitted in any form, electronic or mechanical, including photocopying, recording or by means of any information storage or retrieval system without prior permission in writing from the publishers; or ii) used or reproduced in any way for the training, development or operation of artificial intelligence (AI) technologies, including generative AI technologies. The rights holders expressly reserve this publication from the text and data mining exception as per Article 4(3) of the Digital Single Market Directive (EU) 2019/790.

Bloomsbury Publishing Plc does not have any control over, or responsibility for, any third-party websites referred to or in this book. All internet addresses given in this book were correct at the time of going to press. The author and publisher regret any inconvenience caused if addresses have changed or sites have ceased to exist, but can accept no responsibility for any such changes.

No rights in incidental music or songs contained in the work are hereby granted and performance rights for any performance/presentation whatsoever must be obtained from the respective copyright owners.

All rights whatsoever in this play are strictly reserved and application for performance etc. should be made before rehearsals to Permissions Department, Bloomsbury Publishing Plc, 50 Bedford Square, London, WC1B 3DP, UK. No performance may be given unless a licence has been obtained. No rights in incidental music or songs contained in the Work are hereby granted and performance rights for any performance/presentation whatsoever must be obtained from the respective copyright owners.

A catalogue record for this book is available from the British Library.

A catalog record for this book is available from the Library of Congress.

ISBN: HB: 978-1-3504-9653-8
PB: 978-1-3504-9652-1
ePDF: 978-1-3504-9655-2
eBook: 978-1-3504-9654-5

Series: Methuen Drama Play Collections

Typeset by RefineCatch Limited, Bungay, Suffolk
Printed and bound in Great Britain

For product safety related questions contact productsafety@bloomsbury.com.

To find out more about our authors and books visit www.bloomsbury.com
and sign up for our newsletters.

Content

Introduction 1

Can I Live? by Fehinti Balogun 9
I Am Sending You the Sacred Face by Heather Christian 51
Odds On by Dante or Die 75
To Be a Machine (Version 1.0) by Dead Centre and Mark O'Connell 107
I Hate It Here: Stories from the End of the Old World by Ike Holter 127
every dollar is a soldier/with money you're a dragon by Daniel York Loh 171
T.M. by Ontroerend Goed 191

Note on the Editor 237
Selected Bibliography 239

Introduction

Theatre in the Digital Age: Rehearsals for the Future

Caridad Svich

How to stir up enchantment in a profoundly disenchanted world? How to articulate and parse through the contemporaneous experiences and sudden shocks of a global pandemic and transform them into art? How to dream of a future when it feels as if it has been stolen?

In the early years of the ongoing Covid-19 pandemic, an exceptional and wide range of works made for and/or adapted to transmedia performance tested the boundaries of theatre and challenged ideas about what was possible. While these works sprung from the interpandemic conditions that gave them rise, they also serve as portals for theatre-making's future. While the theatre industry in 2024, at the time of this introduction's writing, is playing a hard game of 'return to normal', there is no denying that humans and other beings are living in the throes of an accelerated planetary emergency combined with an equally accelerated rise in global far-right fascism and necropolitical neoliberalism. In other words, there is no normative return in a pandemicene within the Capitalocene (to use scholar Jason W. Moore's term).[1] The monster, as historian Mike Davis wrote, is not only at the door, but has entered.[2] The planet is already broaching the 1.5 Celsius tipping point,[3] and the 'largest ever recorded leap in the amount of carbon dioxide laden in the world's atmosphere' occurred in May of 2024.[4] Theatre's ability to adapt, change and evolve during the twenty-first century, and thus find a way to survive, will require nimbleness, ingenuity, a practical and material commitment to ecological sustainability, an anti-ableist framing for creation and production, and an openness to making work for multiple play platforms in addition to a greater understanding of how theatre is situated not apart from but within the history of media itself.

Gathered in this collection are the play-scores for seven transmedia theatre pieces made during 2020 and 2022. They are works that have been adapted and/or created for a variety of modalities, as follows: audience-uploaded hybrid performance, one-to-one online interactive work, lip-synch digital musical theatre, climate crisis activist manifesto film/theatre, spoken word installation theatre, interactive game film/theatre, and multi-location broadcast play. What unites them, despite their variance, is a fearless

---

[1] Jason W. Moore, *Anthropocene or Capitalocene? Nature, History, and the Crisis of Capitalism* (Oakland: PM Press, 2016).
[2] Mike Davis, *The Monster Enters: COVID-19, Avian Flu, and the Plagues of Capitalism* (London and Brooklyn: Verso Books, 2020).
[3] Ajit Niranjan, 'Earth on verge of five catastrophic climate tipping points, scientists warn', *The Guardian*, 5 December 2023. https://www.theguardian.com/environment/2023/dec/06/earth-on-verge-of-five-catastrophic-tipping-points-scientists-warn [accessed May 10, 2024].
[4] Oliver Milman, 'Record-breaking increase in CO2 levels in the world's atmosphere', *The Guardian*, 9 May 2024. https://www.theguardian.com/environment/article/2024/may/09/carbon-dioxide-atmosphere-record [accessed May 10, 2024].

exploration of what the site of performance can hold in terms of meaning, affect, liveness and aliveness, synchronous and asynchronous modes, and how presence and co-presence can be re-imagined in transmedia performance. Moreover, most, though not all, of the pieces herein are made by theatre-makers steeped in analogue or semi-analogue creation, and not by longstanding transmedia and/or digital media artists. What you are witnessing, then, in many of these pieces are genuine acts of discovery by these theatre-makers about what is or could be possible in digital and hybrid performance realms. The thrill of discovery, born out of interpandemic necessity, which animates the works herein gives them an extra layer of *frisson*. Whether it is Dead Centre's ingenious decision to upload the audience in *To Be a Machine (Version 1.0)* or Ike Holter's choice to structure his play as a series of sonic tracks in *I Hate It Here*, you are in the presence of the performance, through the technology of the play-text, of a new kind of theatre being made, one that sits among the modalities of cinema, gaming, installation, poetry, sound and video art. It is a theatre that builds upon an already vibrant history of transmedia and inter-medial performance and brings it into direct confrontation with more conventional 'analogue' modes. As such, it is poised at a precipice: one foot in the before times, one foot in the future.

While it is difficult to speak of futurity while one is living through what most scientists acknowledge is the sixth mass extinction,[5] it is still useful to witness how theatre-makers are trying to imagine resilient ways through and forward. At the 2024 Contemporary Drama Conference at the University of Innsbruck, scholar Heidi Liedke, in their keynote address entitled 'Politics of Care in a Digital Age: What Remains after Viral Theatre?', asked the following question: 'How can theatre change the digital?'[6] This is one of the core questions that this collection entreats: How can the languages of theatre change how conventional media modes are thought of, utilized and applied, and what are some of the poetics of transmedia theatre?

Let's face it. Transmedia theatre isn't going away. In fact, it's been here nearly all along.

In 1911 in Berlin, as scholar Steve Dixon states in his landmark book *Digital Performance* (2007), the 'first integration of film within a theatre performance' occurred.[7] This was followed by theatrical experiments in France, the US, Russia and more. Advances in modern technologies – typography, light, sound, photography, and film – have been part of theatre-making always but certainly since electricity was invented. But I do not wish to equate the electronic and digital as an a priori to describe trans-mediation. In his book *Theatre in the Expanded Field* (2013), scholar Alan Read situates the digital on the outer limits of the human body and not merely through 'computing machinery and virtual platforms.'[8] Read focuses his discussion in Chapter Four of his book on the spaces between 'the digital and the technological, a sedimentation of pasts and futures, rather than a succession of stuttering incidents.'[9] While Read's

---

[5] 'Strong evidence shows Sixth Mass Extinction of global biodiversity in progress' (University of Hawaii at Manoa, January 13, 2022). https://www.sciencedaily.com/releases/2022/01/220113194911.htm [accessed May 15, 2024].
[6] Heidi Liedke, from unpublished keynote address, quoted with permission.
[7] Steve Dixon, *Digital Performance* (Cambridge: MIT Press, 2007), p. 73.
[8] Alan Read, *Theatre in the Expanded Field* (London: Bloomsbury, 2013), p. 86
[9] Ibid., p. 110.

remarks in his chapter elucidate (and here I use his analogy) the growing distance that is perceived between the hands of the exhumed body of Lazarus (from the Bible) and the fiber optic filaments that carry the echoes of what is deemed the 'touch' of communication, it is precisely the indeterminate, intangible space illuminated by this distance that can lead us to consider and reconsider the nature and potential of transmedia theatre.

While Liedke in their provocation at the 2024 Contemporary Drama Conference positions the 'digital' mostly in line with the electronic and computational as a definition, what they are getting at in their question of how theatre can change the digital is closer to what Read is stating in his book – namely, how human, fleshy, awkward, messy person-ness can change the perception of supposedly cold, hard, non-fleshy technological elements or spaces. To build on this idea of how transmedia theatre lives in the vibrant fault-lines between and among the physical-corporeal and the data-spectral (my terminology), it is worth looking at the work of Sarah Bay-Cheng, who titled their 2012 essay 'Theater is Media'.[10] In this essay, and in their ongoing, indispensable scholarship on intermediality, Bay-Cheng asks practitioners to position theatre away from the reductive and, I would add, inaccurate binary of theatre (live, analogue) vs. recorded media performance. Instead, they state that 'our notions of theater, dance and performance history [are] influenced by digital processes of recording, storing, writing, retrieving and performing historical documents of performance.'[11] Theatre is not ghosted. It is a ghost already in the machine of the theatre itself! As such, Bay-Cheng continues: 'If media ecology is the study of media', then, 'performance is clearly within this domain as a technology, a technique, a mode of information, a site of numerous codes of communication within human culture.'[12]

Therefore, transmedia theatre lives in the corpo-spectral realm between temporal and atemporal zones, between data storage and the residual memory traces of theatre-makers and audiences (traces that may disrupt or complicate the data's fixed 'nature'), and in the constantly renegotiated spaces of history by and through which theatre and performance are embedded. The play-score, thus, for intermedial performance is also situated between zones. It is an inky, printed (or digital) reminder of the spatial, sceno-graphic, aural-oral-linguistic, inter and intrapersonal geographies traversed by performance. It is both a virtual guide and an emblem of virtuality.

Transmedia theatre's history is vast. Some of its notable figures in the twentieth and early twenty-first century include Robbie McCauley, Laurie Anderson, George Coates, The Wooster Group, Builders Association, Big Art Group, Ping Chong, Mabou Mines, Gob Squad, Jay Scheib, Reza Abdoh, Lola Arias, John Jesurun, Annie Dorsen, Marike Splint, Fake Friends, Theater in Quarantine, Blast Theory, Forced Entertainment, Complicité theatre company, and director Katie Mitchell's pioneering 'live cinema', which began when she staged Virginia Woolf's *The Waves* for the National Theatre in London in 2006. Each of these individual artists or companies have explored and

---

[10] Sarah Bay-Cheng, 'Theater is Media', *Theater* magazine, Volume 42, No. 2 (Duke University Press, 2012).
[11] Ibid., p. 32.
[12] Ibid., p. 34.

disrupted notions of what presence means in intermedial performance. Working with embodiment and disembodiment as co-equal affective 'presences', they have teased audience expectations around and about frameworks of representation. As scholars Gabriella Giannachi, Nick Kaye and Michael Shanks state in their book *Archaeologies of Presence* (2012),[13] presence in transmedia theatre is built upon and within an 'ecology of relationships; in the layered experience of temporality [...] and in the persistence of performance through its representation and archival remains.' The relationship between archival selves and those experienced in 'real' time are further challenged In work that uses real world interfaces as objects of narrative mediation. In 2024, scholars Miriam Felton-Dansky and Jacob Gallagher-Ross coined the term 'interface' theatre to describe precisely plays that show and reflect upon individuals living in a world mediated by interfaces (i.e., text messaging, Google Earth, and more).[14]

Playwriting's history is obviously marked by that of transmedia's past (shall we think back on the *deux ex machina* of classical plays as a mode of machine/mediation?) as well as in its contemporaneity, but pedagogically speaking, plays have often been positioned, from a Western, Anglophone dramatic perspective, in the hard analogue crowd as objects of method and study even after the advent of post-modernism and post-dramatic theatre. Play-texts or play-scores for performance when viewed through the playwright-centred prism, have largely been considered, with few exceptions where the text, for example, has been written directly for online media presentation, like Canadian playwright Jordan Tannahill's *rihannaboi95* (2013), as a priori artifacts for an analogue experience predicated on the concept of shared in person physical time and space. But in the digital age, how do audiences and indeed theatre-makers think about live or performance capture experiences *across* time and space?

Philip Auslander's *Liveness: Performance in a Mediatized Culture* (1999, new editions in 2012 and 2023) changed the discourse in the field when it was first published. Auslander argues not only that performance must be re-thought in the age of mass media but that liveness in and of itself is an evolving concept because it operates through a relational framework. The technologies that form part of an art form and how people relate to them shift how the work is made and viewed. We are in a world where many people on an everyday basis interact with multiple 'user' interfaces – and not just on their phones or laptops. Digital 'billboards' scroll or post text to be read while one is in transit, QR codes link to restaurant menus and healthcare portals, many disabled people rely on robotic or digital apparatuses in order to live, and while there is much necessary chatter about the unethical practices that ground AI language and image-'generating' platforms, it is also true that tools that use elements of artificial intelligence have been and are useful to facilitating automated tasks, especially in the workplace.

When Michael Joyce created his piece *afternoon, story* in 1987 (later published on a diskette by Eastgate Systems in 1990) – one of the first pieces of hypertext literature – he used Storyspace software, which was new at the time and which he co-created, to

---

[13] Gabriella Giannachi, Nick Kaye and Michael Shanks, *Archaeologies of Presence: Art, Performance and the Persistence of Being* (Abingdon and New York: Routledge, 2012), p.11.

[14] Miriam Felton-Dansky and Jacob Gallagher-Ross, 'Interface Theatre: Watching Ourselves Disappear', *Modern Drama*, Volume 67, No.1 (University of Toronto Press, March 2024), pp. 1–24.

craft different lexical pathways for the reader to take on their journey through the story, not unlike a digital promenade performance. This hypertextual mode was presaged in analogue form, in 1963, when Julio Cortazar wrote his novel *Hopscotch*, wherein the reader could choose two different sequences of chapters to affect their experience of the novel's story. Both Joyce and Cortazar understood twenty-four years apart from one another how the affective position of the reader/viewer/participant was key to a sense of a-liveness in the presence of the book in print or online as a technology to be mediated. It holds to reason, thus, that in 2024, just as there are many artists that are reverting or standing by an ontologically 'pristine' reverence for analogous geographic and temporal co-presence as a hierarchically 'better' experience that can be had by an audience (while ignoring that mediation is always part of theatre), many other artists are challenging the co-present relationship between a theatre piece and the audience, including how film can be a site wherein to install a theatre piece! Moreover, whether taking their cues from literary pioneers of electronic literature or artists that have exploring the boundaries between audience and performer in live and digital art, many theatre-makers, including some in this collection, are rethinking the so-called fixed point of view of the audience. Instead, the audience is put in the driver's seat, if you will, to be free to choose how they will interact and play with the piece. Key to this exploration of the audience's agency is less around the immersive nature of works and more to do, curiously, with their aural-spatial dramaturgies. Several of the pieces in this anthology are language and music-driven. The poetics and politics of sound reconfigure the way the play-score's experience lands. How does an audience listen, even if they are multi-tasking, and how is their ear captured by performance?

In considering some of the works created between 2020 and 2022 in the English-speaking theatre for inclusion in this book, I was interested in destabilizing the presumed connection between plays that are about or utilize visible 'technologies' and/or social media applications (i.e. X/Twitter, Meta/Facebook, Snapchat, Google Earth, TikTok, YouTube or platforms created for a specific project) and work that treats the page and potential stage as a technology to be played. Grouping together pieces by lyricist and composer Heather Christian, actor-activist-musician Fehinti Balogun, site-responsive and site-specific company Dante or Die, actor-musician Daniel York Loh, playwright Ike Holter and theatre companies Dead Centre and Ontroerend Goed – all authoring or adapting material in distinctive spatial, aural, scenic, and linguistic registers with equally distinctive relationships with and to an audience – allows one to see a different, less literal relationship to mediated playwriting and theatre-making strategies. If this is the digital age, then how do plays sound and *think* digitally, and how is that thinking expressed in the score for performance that is the game/play-text? Is showing the digital incarnation necessary, or can readers and audiences be asked to imagine?

Putting pieces side by side that approach how they think across media in a variety and sometimes contrapuntal manner opens a different line of enquiry into how the poetics of transmedia performance texts misbehave. I use the word 'misbehave' intentionally, because 'to behave' has been the bane of much of the theatre industry's relationship to playwriting's existence, especially in the West since the rise of the well-made play in the nineteenth century. Plays in the Anglophone world are often judged by critics as to how well they structure their 'beats', create 'rounded' characters, and follow an arc or journey. Plays that don't are, then, misbehaving, and rebelling against the 'rules.' The curious divide that has occurred between plays and performance (and the re-inscription of this 'divide' between theatre studies and performance studies) has started to wane in the last twenty years precisely while the digital and analogue spheres have become more porous in everyday life for able-bodied and disabled people. The porousness has had both positive and negative effects, as it has also coincided with the rise of surveillance capitalism,[15] tech-bro libertarian political alliances with far-right politicians and think tanks, and societies where everything is mined – natural resources of the earth and people's data. But if art reflects life, then it is only natural that theatre-makers are conducting their artistic thought experiments at the intersection of unruly borders and historiographic practices that acknowledge the variety of media, not just social, that affect how humans connect (or not) with one another and the world.

The polycrises of the digital age find their artistic articulations, therefore, in the glitchy mojo that links the failures of the present with the vaulted promise of a stolen future – a future that dreams of a liberatory utopia while moving through the white noise of dystopia. The dramaturgical glitchiness of affect that transmedia theatre tends to revel in, thus, reflects and exposes the fragile, unstable precarity of people and non-human beings living in a world being annihilated by the monsters of fascist and neoliberal 'progress', where, as Daniel York Loh says in his play of the same name, *every dollar is a soldier/with money you're a dragon.*

In this light, it is useful to think about the plays in this collection and how they are situated in contemporaneous theatre through the theoretical framework of two very different yet oddly complementary aesthetic philosophers Paul Virilio and Zygmunt Bauman, whose respective works were popular in the cultural zeitgeist at the advent of transmedia theatre in its late twentieth-century incarnation and into the early noughties. Virilio is best known for articulating, presciently, in *The Administration of Fear* (2012) that 'there is no relationship to terror without a relationship to life and speed. Terror cuts to the quick: it is connected to life and quickness through technology.'[16] Virilio foresaw the dangers of building a socio-political world upon, in part, perpetual communication through computers and the internet at the expense of biological rhythms and seasonal patterns in human and non-human culture. Zygmunt Bauman famously coined the phrase 'liquid modernity' in his book of the same name in 1999,[17] and later in his final book in 2017, referred to the current age as a 'retrotopia'.[18] The 'liquid modern' for Bauman was a move away from a modernity focused on heavy hardware to one focused on light software. Bauman's concerns were with societies that were increasingly rootless and structured against durability. He was attuned to the seductions that the liquid world offered and understood how such a world would increase feelings of uncertainty, and hyper-individualism. In *Retrotopia*, he accurately predicted that instead of a utopia, such a world would devolve into one consumed with nostalgia. This

---

[15] Shoshana Zuboff, *The Age of Surveillance Capitalism* (New York: Public Affairs, Hachette Book Group, 2018).
[16] Paul Virilio with Bertrand Richard, translated by Ames Hodges, *The Administration of Fear*, (Cambridge, MA: Semiotext (e), 2012), p.21.
[17] Zygmunt Bauman, *Liquid Modernity* (Cambridge, MA: Polity Press, 2000).
[18] Zygmunt Bauman, *Retrotopia* (Cambridge, MA: Polity Press, 2017).

'hauntological' world, as re-defined by the influential writer and music critic Mark Fisher was one where people would need to look to relics of the future in the un-activated potentials of the past.[19]

The playwrights and theatre-makers in this collection and many of those working at the philosophical, spiritual, and material intersections between analogue and digital, virtual, and augmented reality modalities, understand that, as Bay-Cheng said, 'theater is media', and that, as media, it is historically positioned within the after-effect of Virilio's naming of a world driven by speed and terror through the retrotopic debris of Bauman's definition of liquid modernity. Building on Mark Fisher's pursuit of a lost future, they are using the socio-technological means of soft power that have been turned against them, and figuratively against the planet itself, to critique, interpret, analyse, re-claim and re-enchant theatre's possibilities. In this they are aligning themselves, consciously or not, with the cyber-queer Black feminist stance taken by cultural theorist Legacy Russell in their book *Glitch Feminism*.[20] Acknowledging the generative aspect of the glitch, the algorithmic errors in the machine, the malfunctions that can be turned into functional apparatuses – the world of illness that can be recovered through a politics of care – this theatre seeks its restoration through fugitive markers and poetically rendered linguistic gleams.

In this collection you will find Dante or Die's fervently soulful *Odds On*, which asks its audience players to take a virtual, meditative gamble with the compulsive addictions of modern life, Ontroerend Goed's deceptively resonant *T.M.*, which crafts a one-to-one live digital experience around questions of ethics and morality, Heather Christian's lip-synch drag musical, written for Theater in Quarantine in New York City, *I Am Sending You the Sacred Face* that demands its audience reckon poetically within the mysteries of Mother Teresa's fallible sainthood, Dead Centre and Mark O'Connell's wry enquiry into trans-humanism and cyborg identity in *To Be a Machine (Version 1.0)*, Ike Holter's multi-locational, multi-vocal funny/sad cry for communal recognition and the necessity of human touch in *I Hate It Here*, Daniel York Loh's incantatory spoken word odyssey through one famous man's (Astor) capitalist success story compared to the unstable migration of un-famous impoverished Chinese people, and Fehinti Balogun's urgent gig/rap/storytelling/lecture documentary film/theatre about climate chaos, and the power of activism to effect change. Each piece, in its own way, finds the human and non-human in the digital, the theatre in performance (and vice versa), and the signs unseen on the portals and interfaces that are the virtual and material fabric of our lives. Themes of repair, resolve, refusal (to be left behind) and recognition reverberate through the plays even as they are separated by their approaches to performance methodology, intention and purpose. They are defiant pieces for a theatre that shouldn't have been theatre, because they were made at a time when theatres went 'dark'. In them, however, there is a light. Media across media, they project the audience and readers into a reconsideration of what the page and its stages can be.

While the works herein are markers of a specific time in performance history, they also point ways forward, not only in terms of form and function, but also in the

---

[19] Mark Fisher, *Ghosts of My Life: Writings on Depression, Hauntology, Lost Futures* (Zero Books, 2022).
[20] Legacy Russell, *Glitch Feminism* (London and Brooklyn: Verso Books, 2020).

challenges and provocations they offer in terms of design, poetics, and the exploration of the text-site(s)-audience relationship. Thinking digitally, they enact corporeal magic. Their lessons are ones of grief and hope because they recognize that all theatre is a dance between life and death. Mortal games haunt the direct encounters and phantasmagoric reveries on these pages. Extinction is close. But not yet. Haunted against and within hauntology, transmedia plays bust open normative practices of theatre-making, or better put, transmedia plays *play*.

Can I Live?

Fehinti Balogun

A digital performance about the climate catastrophe conceived, written, and performed by Fehinti Balogun. Weaving his story with spoken word, rap, theatre, animation and scientific facts, the play/film invites audiences to recognize that they are not alone in facing and addressing the planetary emergency.

Can I Live? was first performed and filmed at the Barbican Theatre, London, in 2021. It is a Complicité production in association with the Barbican, supported by Oxford Playhouse. After its filming, it toured digitally from September 2021 onwards.

Fehinti Balogun is an actor, theatre-maker and activist. British born, Nigerian raised, Balogun is best known for his work in the films *Dune* (2021), *The Bastard Son & The Devil Himself* (Netflix, 2022), *Juliet, Naked* (2018) and the TV series *I May Destroy You* on HBO and BBC One (2020) and *A Gentleman in Moscow* (2024). He starred in Amy Berryman's play *Walden* (2021) in the West End.

From the Author: On *Can I Live?*

In 2017 Kirsty Housley and Matt Hartley cast me in a play at the Royal Shakespeare Company called *Myth*. It was a modern farce-like comedy about the climate crisis. Now, at this point I had no idea about the climate crisis, other than lacklustre geography lessons on the subject and James Cameron's *Avatar* (2009) – but boy would I in the months to come. After doing the research for the part, I did what most people do when discovering climate crisis – I sunk into panic mode, becoming unable to function properly in a world that's refusing to acknowledge how big the problem is. The next two years would be spent managing the anxiety with little actions like cutting out meat or recycling. As you could imagine, that did very little to change our overall situation and therefore didn't do all that much to change my anxiety. We live in a world that has no framework to help us to understand the enormity of the climate crisis, structurally or culturally. And attempts at individual actions just weren't doing what we hoped they would.

I realized I needed to be part of a collective to achieve anything or at the very least be around people who felt like I did. But when I joined movements like XR (extinction rebellion) the people I saw in the in meeting rooms and protesting on the streets very rarely reflected me or my experiences.

And then, even with all the success around changing public understanding, none of it made my mum feel any better about my involvement with it all. In fact, she felt hurt, that I, her son would put himself in danger like that. With how hard she has worked in her life there theoretically should be no reason I would put myself in harm's way. Where I saw myself as part of the movement on the front line my mother saw her baby boy, a Black boy, putting himself amid danger surrounded by people who did not understand that when it comes to these kinds of situations 'the way they treat us is different'.

My mum and I argued back and forth for many weeks. On our last confrontation, I secretly placed my phone under a pillow and recorded the whole thing. I wanted to understand her point of view, outside of what was bound to be an emotional interaction. I also wanted evidence that she would inevitably go on to deny – 'no, Fehinti, you don't remember that correctly'. But, when listening back to the recordings, I realised I had never really listened her point of view. I like so many others, did not take her experience into account. These voice recordings became a lecture centred around both hers and my experiences. A lecture that later went on to become this play *Can I Live?* Hold tight Abraham for Title inspiration.

The play is an amalgamation of all my experiences coming into the climate work, starting our story in the height of the pandemic in lockdown 2020. Most of the experiences and interactions speeches dialogue are inspired by real life experiences.

The play is heavily inspired by Childish Gambino's 'This Is America' music video (2018), a 1-shot music video directed by Hiro Murai that takes you from world to world all in the same space. Music and dancing is also at the centre of this piece, it helps move these ideas from just our heads to a whole body, bringing joy and hope to the experience of it all.

When developing the piece, I never thought it would be published, as it was so visual and elements central to its understanding were worked out physically in the long workshop phase. So, I have attempted to add a few more descriptions to give you, the reader, more of a feeling of how it worked. Each new heading in the text is adapted from the original headings in the lecture. These headings were indicators that there needed to be a change of energy or movement in the space, especially in the first section, where we really must keep the audience's attention. We had had an amazing creative team with us to work this all out. From Kirsty Housley, the woman who first introduced me to the subject and then later became the dramaturg of this piece to our amazing co-directors Daniel Bailey and Simon McBurney, to our brilliant musicians like Khalil Madovi and TEE to name just a few.

When we originally workshopped, we kept challenging ourselves to just play. To use all the disparate aspects of my life in this time of activism to help people along the journey of understanding all these massive themes. From the poems I had written to cope which later became songs, to the artwork in my home that inspired the set and clothing we used in the piece.

The first principle I use in climate communications is to 'meet them where they're at.' You cannot expect someone to care about something as much as you do as quickly as you hope. It takes time, sometimes like building a beach from a cliff, years' worth of erosion, with sustained and consistent contact. And on this journey we thought about that. How do we meet people where they are? it is hard to scare/ blame someone into action. That energy becomes unsustainable in the long term. However, to share (acknowledging that to share is one of the bravest things we as humans can do) is a vastly different thing. To share one's experience in its fullest and invite people to see aspects of themselves in your work creates change. It's no longer about blaming or shaming or telling someone they're doing something wrong. When you share you invite them to go on the journey with you, to challenge themselves as they see you do the same, to see and feel the imperfect journey. That is why so much of *Can I Live?* is real, and why I cast my real mother in the piece to speak some of her own words, which she'd originally spoken in the voice recordings I had taken of our arguments. All to show my belief that Hope the verb (the thing we constantly sustain with action, community and vison) is more sustainable than fear or blame.

I hope you enjoy *Can I Live?* and that it inspires you and helps you with your artistic contribution to the world or understanding of the climate crisis. It was our aim that it should feel like a mixture between a theatre show, stand-up and live gig, so please keep that in mind as you read.

I would like to thank the amazing people in my life for helping me create this, from those that first watched the lecture and gave me notes, to the those that heard my early bars, and encouraged me to keep going. You know who you are. Thank you. And, as always, thank you Mum.

Enjoy.

Fehinti Balogun

Can I Live?

Can I Live? was first performed and filmed at the Barbican Theatre, London, in 2021. It is a Complicité production in association with the Barbican, supported by Oxford Playhouse. After its filming, it toured digitally from September 2021 onwards. The original cast and creative team was as follows:

Cast

Fehinti	**Fehinti Balogun**
Deji	**Kwami Odoom**
Kwami	**Khalil Madovi**
Mum	**Bunmi Adedeji**
Grandma	**Ellen Thomas**
Ken Saro-Wiwa	**Fehinti Balogun**
Policeman	**Fehinti Balogun**
Government MP	**Fehinti Balogun**
Chloe	**Chloe Rianna**
Dickson	**Dickson Mbi**
Tee	**Tee**

Director	Daniel Bailey
Co-Director	Simon McBurney
Dramaturg	Kirsty Housley
Producer	Tim Bell
Director of Photography	Stewart Kyasimire (Create Anything)
Editor	Ash J. Woodward
Scenography	Rajha Shakiry
Costume Design	Rajha Shakiry
Music Director & Composer	Khalil Madovi
Sound Design	Mike Winship
Lighting Design	Azusa Ono
Movement Director	Dickson Mbi
Projection, Animation & Visual Effects Design	Ash J. Woodward
Activists	Nick Anim, Helen Brewer, Sara Callaway, Samia Dumbuya and Joshua Virasami
Music	Fehinti Balogun, Tee, Khalil Madovi, Chloe Rianna and Josh Sneesby

Can I Live? was supported by Arts Council England, Calouste Gulbenkian Foundation (UK Branch) and Doc Society Climate Story Fund.

SECTION 1: Introduction to Fehinti and home

Fehinti's *home is a typical council house living room, made a home. Nigerian art hangs on yellow walls. Small African sculptures are dotted around, amongst family pictures – some in traditional dress, some more casual, and some school photos. We are viewing him through a Zoom call. As the Zoom room fills,* **Fehinti** *is doing various things to warm up: sit-ups, push-ups, vocal exercises, etc. For us, the audience, it is a montage of activity, intersected with a flurry of music and credits . . . until we finally settle on* **Fehinti***, sitting on the floor, leaning on his sofa. Behind is a blanket and pillows. This is his world.*

Fehinti   Hey, hello. OK, two seconds.

I'm just . . . I'm moving stuff around. I'm with you.

Hi, hi my name is Fehinti Balogun, welcome to my home! Well, actually, not my home, my mum's home. I came here at the beginning of lockdown AND . . . I am still here, yay. I set up my bed at night and then I pack it up in the morning, coz you know, it's a communal space and it's been, well. Yeah, humbling, mad humbling.

Phone pings.

Sugar. Hold on. Oh it's from my brother wishing me luck for this, hold on.

Speaks into phone recording voice note.

Hey, T, yeah, um. I'm just doing the project right now actually. Yeah, I will give you a bell back. Thank you, for all the love. All right, peace and love, love, love bye.

Um actually my brother came here at the beginning of lockdown too – and as he just texted me. I feel like we should give him a little shout-out. So this is a picture of my brother from a couple years ago.

He holds up his phone showing a family picture – the boys are young and sweet.

That's him right there, little cutie . . . And this is him now.

He holds up his phone again – this photo is of his brother looking like a model. It's very cool and edgy.

Ridiculous! I'm actually trying to live my life like he looks. In fact in this next family picture, my brother looks like a mumble rapper, my mum looks like his manager, and I look like a fan trying to get a selfie.

He holds up his phone again – this is another family picture, but now the brother looks like a rap star not wanting to be photographed.

I'm actually genuinely, palpably jealous.

SECTION 2: A walk to the shop and plastic bags

And being home has made me revert to a younger version of myself – petulant, moody. And one day, one hot day, my moody ol' self and mum decide to walk up to the shops to see if they have a yam and plantain. I'd been craving it, we both had. We were two months in without it at this point, so we brave it. We step out the door, it's peak lockdown one, right? We're met by at least ten of my neighbours having a street party. I was mad, but my mum, she didn't want to make a fuss and just wanted to ignore it, not cause trouble. But I was mad, man. I mean, I'm not going to let it stop me getting my plantain, but . . .

Anyway, we're going up the hill and my mum's back starts to hurt, so we slow down, and I'm like, 'Mum you know if you did your stretches it wouldn't be this bad'. And she's over hearing me saying this, but I say 'it's not going to get any better unless we do something'. But she's tired, man. She was working a more than 9–5 job in a bedroom/office, that she barely got to leave. Who am I to say anything?

Anyway, we get to the shop, and the guy at the till, the cashier, he hands us plastic bags. Again, Mum is like 'It's fine', and I'm like, 'No it's not, we have bags, we brought bags.'

The two of them side-step my annoyance. My mum saying with half a smile, 'Ah, he's trying to save the planet', she takes the bags and hands me the shopping.

The guy at the till is, smile-laughing like, 'Ah, yeah man, saving the planet and dat. That's good man' – Prick – 'Yeah man, I wish I had paper bags, but you know, we have to use the plastic, that's all we got.'

Right

'It's like, what am I supposed to do?'

We walk out in total silence.

No, I didn't do my usual thank you smile. My, 'thank you for not seeing me as an inconvenience' smile.

I was pissed the fuck off.

Halfway down the hill I just burst. 'Don't just laugh at me even when it comes to plastic bags, Mum. I do all this work talking to people who, at the end of the day, just laugh it off, side-step the issue. Like you just did!'

SECTION 3: This changes everything

He moves the camera to the table and starts to play with his food.

I start to feel useless. How am I, a person trapped in my family home, supposed to do anything to help the climate crisis? Or quite frankly any issue outside of: have I showered today and can I eat rice for the third time? You can.

A spoon full of jollof is brought into frame.

And as I eat my food, I'm reminded, God, plantain is God's gift to mankind. I'll die on that hill, don't care what anyone says. Also, did you know, because of the increase in heat and dryness in Cameroon, they suffered a 43 per cent decrease in plantain yield? Plantain.

Can I Live?   17

Eats plantain.

I'm angry, man. Not at that man who sold me plastic bags. I'm stuck, thinking about everyone and everything because . . .

This will change everything. The lives of normal people working to feed their kids.

cough excuse me. (*Picks up water.*)

Underscore for the song begins subtly.

People just going to Tesco's to do their weekly shop. Year 11s sitting their GCSEs . . . And for what?

SECTION 4: The life I was promised

He leaves the laptop on the table and moves out into the space.

    I'm drawn to think of the life I was promised
    And if I'm honest
    These promises seem dishonest.

    Coz I ain't got it
    Feel like can't stop it
    They're dishonest
    Choking on lies I'm coughing.

    See, I'm living a version of the truth that lets me carry on
    I have an aversion of the truth so I can carry on
    Keep calm and carry on.

    Man, it's long
    I'm looking for a champion
    Can't handle pressure
    We avoid, here in Albion
    Leaders hunt the money
    And the money-feeling, really strong
    Well you can't eat money, so anxiety's coming on
    Money's just paper
    And the paper's just trees
    And the burning of the trees brings breathing to its knees.

    I'm drawn to think of the life I was promised
    And if I'm honest
    These promises seem dishonest.

    I'm drawn to think of the life I was promised
    And if I'm honest
    These promises seem dishonest.

Flip a coin an' toss it,
Coz the outcome is abhorrent
If we see it we could stop it
But I feel it, it's not stopping.

Brain rocking
Trying to find a solution.
Well yeah, recycling is as dead as pollution

And yeah, reduction is the truth of the movement.
The system is too fucked up to do it.
The people trying to live and get through it.
Worry about the weeks
when it's years that we're losing.
Water drying up, it's the food that they've screwed with.
Life's not a game but I feel like I'm losing.
Gaslit by ignorance, it's ignorance some are choosing.

The countries that pollute the most, tend to get richer.
They leave a model, how to do it, messing up the picture.
Picture's set, bare doubt, are we getting through it?
I'm not a scientist but clearly there is something to it.

I'm drawn to think of the life I was promised
And if I'm honest
These promises seem dishonest.

I'm drawn to think of the life I was promised
And if I'm honest
These promises seem dishonest.

SECTION 5: Climate crisis

Listen, this graph right here, hold on.

He shows a graph via screensharing. The graph is an animation showing increases in temperature all over the globe.

Yeah, so this graph is taken from the National Aeronautics and Space Administration, otherwise known as NASA. It shows us the increase in temperature abnormalities from 1900 to 2020.

It shows us the continents of /North America, South America, Europe, Asia, Africa and Australasia.

The redder the line becomes, the more extreme the abnormalities and what they'll mean. And as our overall temperature increases, there will be a rise in these abnormalities in our weather, water and food supplies.

The red lines have grown to be extreme for each country.

I want to make something really clear: I am not a scientist.

He stops screen sharing.

But there is very clearly something wrong.

This is a climate crisis.

SECTION 6: Two acts of bravery

With the pandemic and the year we have had, a lot has been asked of us – to come together, to sacrifice, to be brave.

So, I would like to talk about bravery.

Let's shift you here.

Fehinti *moves his computer screen. In the background we see family pictures on the wall.* **Mum** *and boys. Baby pictures, aunties and uncles. New underscore starts.*

From a very early age, these people, my family, taught me three principles. Some of these principles you may recognize.

They were: to keep your head down; do your work; and don't get into trouble.

And it makes sense, right? The payoff is in the thing you create with all your years of hard work of staying in your lane, staying out of trouble.

And in African culture, it's almost directly related to certain career paths. Some of these career paths you may recognize. They are the doctor, the lawyer and the businessman.

Fehinti *holds up badly edited photos of his face cropped onto people doing these jobs – doctor, lawyer, businessman.*

So, my first act of bravery was rebelling against these choices.

I wanted to be an actor. 'Why do you want to prostitute your emotions for money? How can you safeguard your future without a proper degree?' was my mum's first reaction.

But the more she learned, the more she got behind me.

Because, bro, I was given a new consciousness. I could be an actor. However, there were people within my education system that told me I might not get into drama school because, well . . . they might already have so many people of colour.

There is always a moment where you come up against a system that is calibrated in a way that unjustly affects you. And, because it's a system, you're not allowed to say anything.

I bet there's been a moment in your life where you rebelled against a system or a way of thinking because you knew it was wrong. Like being stopped and searched and asking why, or calling out a colleague for the way they spoke to you. 'No, Sarah, you can't touch my hair.'

It's in these moments that something in us makes us brave. Makes us rebel.

My second act of bravery was . . .

Telling my mum I got involved with environmental activism.

As you can imagine that went . . . well . . .

Look, I'd just learned about the crisis, and I was surrounded by people that didn't feel like me.

Yeah, me and my mum, we talked. And by talked, I mean argued.

I wasn't keeping my head down. I wasn't staying in my lane. I wasn't staying out of trouble. But that is the only way I knew how to safeguard our future.

SECTION 7: Fehinti's tipping point

Fehinti *picks up the camera and turns it 90 degrees to face the wall, placing it on a higher surface.* **Fehinti** *is now standing. We can see him from the waist up, and his full body as he goes further to the back wall.*

See, in 2018, we'd just had one of the hottest summers in history, after having one of the hottest summers in history. And for the first time I could see it. I could feel it. Fields in London turning brown. Crops across the continent were dying. And I did the only thing I knew how to do in this moment of panic.

I turned to Twitter.

A tweet sound accompanies every tweet projected on the background. All of these are **Fehinti***'s real life tweets and memes from internet activism. Some calling out government investments, some trying to work out where the money is coming from, and other government failures.*

I tweeted and I tweeted and I tweeted.

I wrote to my local MP and, as you can imagine, nothing happened.

I felt alone and small and powerless.

And then I was told about climate activism.

People who understood how bad things were, and that not enough was being done.

Non-violent civil disobedience. The road blocking. The sitting down to stand up.

Music.

> These groups dey do feel like you
> Groups they do feel like you
> These groups dey do feel like you. (x3)

SECTION 8

The music takes over, its afro beats infecting **Fehinti**'s *whole body, pulsing through him.*

> These groups dey do feel like you
> Groups they do feel like you
> These groups dey do feel like you. (x4)

We play with the music coming in and out, the room is full of images and videos of protesters projected on the wall, dancing. The energy is electric, it's like he is on the streets with them.

> Now I wasn't keen to get arrested
> Blocking roads that was contested
> The veins of our streets, they were congested
> It's the first time I saw the system bested.
>
> You cannot get from A to B
> If you cannot get past me
> So now you see
> The problem.
>
> We have to look so we can solve them.
> We have to look so we can . . .
>
> Look to the left look, to the right
> I'm feeling alright
> I'm feeling alright.
>
> These groups dey do feel like you
> Groups they do feel like you
> These groups dey do feel like you.
>
> Look to the left look, to the right
> I'm feeling alright
> I'm feeling alright.
>
> These groups dey do feel like you
> Groups they do feel like you
> These groups dey do feel like you.

In a study of successful movements, led by Harvard Professor Erica Chenowith, she found that whenever 3.5 per cent of the population have joined a movement, it's succeeded, and often with far less.

Three point five per cent.

So I joined the movement.

I found things to do that were crucial, but had nothing to do with the police. The admin bits, the sending emails, making calls. Lecturing, talking about my experience. And then braving it, and attending a protest.

But whilst in these meeting rooms, whilst on these protests, a question loomed in my mind.

SECTION 9: Why don't these people look like me?

Why don't these people look like me?

Music cuts out completely.

See, the climate movement for the last thirty years seems to have been white and middle-class. And it feels like it's been like that forever. So, what – do people like me not know? Do we not care?

A recorded voice, **Fehinti**'s *friend* **Kwami**, *plays without prompt. As it does,* **Fehinti** *moves the camera back to the table.*

Kwami   Yeah, I feel like when it comes down to it . . .

Fehinti   This is a recording of my friend Kwami – what he had to say when we talked about this.

Kwami   Yeah, I feel like when it comes down to it, it's about money. My mum's at work, you know what I mean? She doesn't have time to get to grips with all that, or get the eco stuff.

Fehinti   Right, so there is privilege to the environmental fight. I'm talking about those who have the money to buy the eco stuff, have the time to protest, have the privilege to think about anything else but surviving.

SECTION 10: Racism in policing/survival

People of colour experience barriers to the forefront of the climate movement, and I feel like they come from the underlying principles of survival. It's proven statistically.

Like me, Fehinti Balogun. I am four times more likely to have force used against me if I am arrested than my white counterpart.

I'm eight times more likely to be stopped and searched than my white counterpart. And if you're a person of colour, you are four times more likely.

And even though I am statistically less likely to use drugs, I am statistically more likely to be charged for drug possession.

This fear is real.

The fear is legitimized. The bias causes death. The deaths prompt outrage. The outrage brings protest for the sake of imminent survival.

SECTION 11: Ken moment 1

Sudden change of lighting, flash transition representing change of place. **Fehinti** *turns quickly in position. We are now in a car. Police lights flashing, sirens to follow them. Crickets and other noises representing a warm night in Nigeria. We are somewhere else now in the darkness of night.*

Ken   Suddenly, my car screeched to a halt. An armed security man is flagging the car down with his rifle.

Police *(V/O)*   Get out of your car.

Ken   I am not getting out.

Silence.

Police *(V/O)*   Tell your driver to follow us.

Ken   Where are we going to?

Pan in on the face.

Snap back to living room. On the chair again.

SECTION 12: Studio reveal

Fehinti *stands and walks to the edge of the room.*

We are in crisis.

The extreme weather we are having is set to increase. The hot days will continue to get hotter and drier and, although in this country that might seem like a great thing, it really isn't. Especially when you consider food and crops.

The things we need to survive can't survive these extreme weather changes. Floods followed by extreme drought. The spreading of disease.

The door behind **Fehinti** *opens,* **Deji** *walks in and hands* **Fehinti** *his jacket.*

Deji   Yo, Fey, I think you'll need your coat.

Fehinti   Thanks, bro, appreciate that.

Obviously, honestly, I'm not actually at home. I'm in a studio, with a crew . . .

Fehinti *turns his eyes from the Zoom camera to a second camera, and the shot changes. We now see clearly that* **Fehinti** *is inside a set, on a stage. The camera follows* **Fehinti** *as he moves out of the living room set and into the stage. The theatre stage is revealed, complete with camera operators, directors, sound crew equipment and a band – the space is much much bigger than we've been led to believe.*

Fehinti *greets the band, the camera panning to each member in turn, saying hello.*

   . . . and a band . . . Boy, you better stop, you know you're looking good, G.

Tee My Man.

Tee, *the bassist, smiles.*

Fehinti Chloe Riana let's gooo.

Chloe Yes surr

Fehinti *and* **Chloe**, *the drummer, do an intricate fist bump.*

Fehinti Kwams, you're looking good boi.

Kwami *is on keyboards – he knows he looks good. They dab/ handshake.*

Fehinti *turns to the camera.*

All here to help. So let's start from the beginning. What is climate change?

Lights dim, piano plays. **Fehinti** *puts his hands together and pulls them apart, there is light between them.*

SECTION 13: Mum intervention

Phone rings.

Oh my goodness, I am so sorry. Um, literally two seconds, just keep . . .

Fehinti *answers, turning away from the camera, but we hear the conversation. As he moves through the space, we follow. We see everyone getting on with their jobs in the background: band tuning instruments, playing little riffs; crew moving set; directors waiting for the show to start again. We take it all in, as we slowly catch up with* **Fehinti**.

Fehinti Hello?

Mum (*on phone*)   Fehinti, please tell me, why is your bag in my hallway? Do you want me to die?

Fehinti No.

Mum Leaving your things je-je, I am not a young woman oh. You cannot come and kill me. Come and move your things.

Fehinti This is not the time. I can't, I'm doing my environmental project, you know the thing I told you about, do you remember?

Mum You're not recruiting people, Fehinti?

Beat.

I saw on your Facebook, you just popped up, because, I, I wasn't checking, but somebody made a comment about what was going on. A Protester. Yes, it's good, but it's on social media, you understand what I'm saying?

Fehinti Yeah, yeah, yeah.

Can I Live?   25

Mum   It is detrimental to your career. I don't . . . these people! What I'm trying to say if the worst comes to the worst, yeah? What happens for them, will be different to what happens for you. You understand?

Fehinti   Yes, I understand.

Mum   Do you understand, Fehinti?

Fehinti   Yes, Mum, look, I understand that they make really difficult decisions but for a reason. Look can we talk about this later?

Mum   OK. just clean up after yourself, Fehinti.

Fehinti   OK, all right, good, thank you, thank you, bye!

Fehinti *hands the phone to* **Kwami**.

Fehinti *turns back to the camera.*

I am so sorry, but look, let's just – let's start from the beginning, yeah? Yeah.

SECTION 14: What is climate change?

What is climate change?

Again the lighting dims. Piano music starts up. **Fehinti** *claps his hands together and pulls them apart, a spark of light is created that grows to become a large sun. He then places it in the corner of the screen.* **Fehinti** *then creates an earth to sit alongside it just below the middle of the screen under his chest. The background has gone to complete darkness with stars twinkling in the background.*

See, the sun emits heat towards the planet. The heat warms up our planet and then it's released into space.

Fehinti *clicks his fingers showing the movement of heat from animated sun to animated earth.*

However, on its way out, it is massively held up by greenhouse gases we hold in our atmosphere. The more greenhouse gases we have, the longer our planet hugs this heat. Meaning our planet gets hotter and hotter.

We burn huge amounts of fossil fuels, in every aspect of our lives.

In fact, in the last fifty years we have added more greenhouse gases in the air than we have done for the last 800,000 years.

And that increase started not too long ago.

Fehinti *stands over the animated earth he created; factories appear as he moves his hands over it.*

In the eighteenth century, we began the Industrial Revolution, the period in which Europe and America moved from making products with their hands and tools to using mass machinery and factories.

SECTION 15: The more the emissions

Music begins.

And so our rise in CO2 emissions began.

> The more emissions,
> The hotter it gets.
> I said, the more emissions,
> The hotter it gets.
>
> Often, we talk about 1.5 and 2 degree increases in temperature. But what do we mean?
> We mean the average of the heat of the entire globe
> Even the places that are mostly covered up with snow
> Now 1.5 don't seem a lot
> It's an average temperature, it gets really hot
>
> Why?
> The more emissions,
> The hotter it gets.
> I said, the more emissions,
> The hotter it gets.

(*Loop.*)

> Often, we talk about 1.5 and 2 degrees increase in temperature. But what do we mean?
> We mean the average of the heat of the entire globe
> Even the places that are mostly covered up with snow
> Now 1.5 don't seem a lot
> It's an average temperature, it gets really hot
>
> Why?
>
> Coz the more emissions
> The hotter it gets.
> I said the more emission
> The hotter it gets. (x3)

The animated earth moves away and **Fehinti** *dances in front of the band. It's wild fun, almost krumping. The music then ends and* **Fehinti** *drops out of frame.*

SECTION 16: We are in fever

We pan down to **Fehinti**. *The sofa has appeared behind him. As we zoom out further, we reveal* **Deji** *is sitting on the sofa too.*

Fehinti   See, an easier way to imagine these huge shifts in temperature is to imagine the human body.

Deji   OK.

Fehinti   So, take a hand, go on.

Deji   Mm-hmm.

Fehinti   Feel the person underneath that hand. The heartbeat, the history. See, the average human body temperature sits somewhere between 36.5 degrees and 37.5 degrees. As soon as you go below 36.5 degrees, you're on your way to hypothermia. And when you go above 37.5 degrees, you're on your way to fever.

Because of this massive increase in greenhouse gases, the average global temperature has increased 1.1 Celsius since 1880. We are in fever.

SECTION 17: Impact in the UK / Class crisis

In this section a sutble orchestral cinematic underscore plays. Projections of fire and then floods take over **Deji**'s *body. It is beautiful and devastating.*

And we are already experiencing more climate extremes, whole seasons in a week. This country had more wildfires in 2019 than any other year in pre-summer records, some raging for over a fortnight.

And, because of this extreme heat, the warm air holds more water moisture. Meaning more than a month's worth of rain in just a few hours.

Flash floods washing away roads, destroying houses across the UK.

And this flooding, well, it's directly linked to our loss in crops. Cauliflower prices have soared. Cabbage, broccoli and brussels sprouts – they're also in short supply.

The shorter the supply of food the more expensive it becomes, directly affecting the people that find it hard to afford that food in the first place.

The climate crisis is a class crisis.

SECTION 18: Mum intervention 2 / Gran's birthday

Phone rings – music and projection fades.

Fehinti   That's not me, I switched off my phone.

Deji   It's not me.

The **Cameraman** *looks at his phone.*

Fehinti   No, mate, just take it, it's fine.

Cameraman   Fehinti, it's your mum.

Hands the phone to **Fehinti**.

Fehinti   What?

(*Speaks into phone.*)   Hello?

Mum (*on phone*)   Fehinti? Did you not see my text?

Fehinti   NO, I – How did you get this number?

Mum   Have you called your grandma?

Fehinti   No, I haven't – I cannot keep pausing.

Mum   She will switch off her phone for prayers, and then she'll be in church all night. I'm calling now.

Fehinti   No, no, no, no!

Switches to video call.

Fehinti   Happy birthday, Grandma!

Grandma   Oh, my son, I am fine.

Fehinti   Good, good, good.

Grandma   When am I coming to your wedding? I do not want to leave this earth without seeing you married.

Fehinti   Hahahahah. OK!

Grandma   Why are you laughing? I will pray for you. Everything will be OK. Marry whoever you like, but if it is a Oyibo woman, make sure she's Irish, or she understands.

Fehinti   Understands what, Ma?

Grandma   Understands what we mean when we talk about history. Your mummy sent me a picture of you. Handsome boy!

Fehinti   Hahaha. Stop it, stop it! Keep going!

Grandma   What is it with the hair, what is happening?

Fehinti   Oh, I'm just growing it ma, can you see?

Grandma   Bush boy! Hahahahaha. My hippie grandson! Hahaha

Fehinti   OK, I am going to leave you two to it, I love you, Grandma. Happy birthday, bye, bye, bye.

Grandma   Don't forget what I said, I don't want to see God without coming to your wedding.

Fehinti   All right, Grandma, bye, bye bye! Love you, bye, bye bye!

Ends call.

SECTION 19: Family

The sofa is now gone. The space is empty but is being filled with a projection of a family tree made of spirits, flowing from **Fehinti***'s feet, extending to the wall. Each one is a member of* **Fehinti***'s family. It's visually stunning.*

See, my grandma met my grandfather when they were both just children. And when my grandfather became of age, he moved to London to become an accountant. When my grandmother sought something new, she moved to London.

And after months and months of him charming her, they got married and they had my mother, and my aunty.

Music kicks in hard, full drum solos and sax flurries. As **Fehinti** *moves with the music, we see his family tree projection moving and dancing too. He walks into his history.*

> Then they moved back to Nigeria
> Where they had
> Three more kids
>
> So we had
> My uncle
> And my aunty
> And my aunty
> And my aunty
> And my mum.
>
> And again.
>
> That's my uncle
> And my aunty
> And my aunty
> And my aunty
> And my mum. (x3)
>
> Come on, come on!
>
> That's my uncle
> And my aunty
> And my aunty
> And my aunty
> And my mum.
>
> Come on, come on!
>
> That's my uncle
> And my aunty
> And my aunty

And my aunty
And my mum.

That's my uncle. Ahhh
Yes, that is my uncle . . .
Ahhh

One more time.
That's my uncle
And my aunty
And my aunty
And my aunty
And my mum.

And again.
That's my uncle
And my aunty
And my aunty
And my aunty
And my mum.

One more time!
That's my uncle
And my aunty
And my aunty
And my aunty
And my mum.

Music cuts abruptly. The family disappears and is replaced by red and yellow light. A room of fire.

SECTION 20: What's happening in Nigeria

Fehinti *speaks to camera.*

Currently, in Nigeria, we are losing 350,000 hectares of land per year due to drought and desertification. That's 1,544 Olympic parks, or 1,351 square miles a year lost.

Why don't we talk about the poisoning of rivers and streams by Shell, or the British colonial assault on Nigerian oil since 1905?

How can just less than half the population live in extreme poverty, when Nigeria is the biggest oil exporter in Africa?

Why don't we talk about the fact they make huge pillars of fire you can see from space, by burning the excess natural gas, around communities without electricity or running water.

Can I Live? 31

This 'excess gas' could be used to meet the electrical needs of the entire country.

So, why doesn't my mum, or my aunty, or my uncle, or my aunty, or my aunty, or my mum, or my grandma talk about it?

SECTION 21: Why don't we talk about it?

The beat drops and **Fehinti** *is taken by music again, feeling the chorus take over. This is full rap video. The camera is being pushed and pulled away. Cutting between dancing and rapping. 808 and trumpets.*

Music.

> Why don't we talk about it?
> Why don't we talk about it?
> Why don't we
> Why don't we
> Why don't we talk about it?
> Why don't we talk about it?
>
> Why don't we talk about it? Why I have to search Google just to find out it's there? I swear
> Conspiracy coming and growing thicker than Nigerian hair
> Like oooh
> I'm the first to know if Nigeria building a stadium there
> Last to know about flooding the desserts that come in
> They changing the air.
>
> Like woo
>
> Why don't we talk about it?
> Why don't we talk about it?
> Why don't we
> Why don't we
> Why don't we talk about it?
> Why don't we talk about it?
>
> I'm watching them burn the house down.
>
> Look at me trying
> Thirty years we have been trying
> Look at my people they're dying
> Coastal islands, they are dying.
>
> All that money in the Trident
> Wrath coming down like Poseidon
> Flood me in like an island.

Forget me now like the Mayans
Prophecies, they are not silenced.

Woo

Why don't we talk about it?
Why don't we talk about it?
Why don't we
Why don't we
Why don't we talk about it?
Why don't we talk about it?

Ancestors did their best
Information lacking, it's a stress
All covered up, let's undress
Hell fires ain't
Heaven sent.

It hit me.

The people affected
Are feeling dejected
Are not the ones keeping busy.

The spin on this shit
Is doing its bit
It's making me feel dizzy.

It's making me feel dizzy.

The beat and ancestors fade away.

SECTION 22: Climate change is modern-day colonialism

Some of these words appear on the screen as **Fehinti** *speaks them.*

It hit me. Nigeria pollutes almost ten times less per capita than England. Bangladesh is similar too.

America emits 100 times more than Madagascar, one of our most at-risk countries.

It seems to me, some of the people who are the most affected are the ones who have been historically stolen from.

Climate change is modern colonialism.

SECTION 23: Where the wealth was stolen from

In this section **Fehinti** *becomes a full black and white animation.*

I mean, I talked to you about the Industrial Revolution
Where big things took hold like our mass pollution
Great wealth came along, no that's not the solution
But where that wealth came from, now there's the intrusion.

Drum beat kicks in.

> The wealth starts amassing back in 1760
> When it started back then cotton got really nifty
> Machinery used the wool, but the cotton was better
> Whatever the weather, the cotton, it came together.
>
> From the cushion to the lining, from the lining to the clothes
> Where it came from, not everybody knows.
>
> The cotton came from bloody hands
> Came from the pain and contempt
> A generation whose freedom came and went.
>
> It was slavery,
> All amassed in slavery.
> Wait, that's just America?
> Now thinking that amazes me.
>
> It was slavery,
> All amassed in slavery.
> Wait, that's just America?
> Now thinking that amazes me.
>
> Slavery plantations in the Caribbean
> In the Caribbean.
>
> Slavery plantations in the Caribbean
> In the Caribbean.

Slavery plantations in the Caribbean provided the raw material needed for industrial change and growth in the British Empire.

> But it goes deeper.
>
> Fused with that history of slavery
> Are the genocides and the conquests.

Cut music.

> The liberation of oil by liberators
> That deliberate the price of liberation
> Whilst polluting all the soil.

Shout out to Shell.

An animated hand picks up soil, this becomes **Fehinti**'s *real hand. We zoom out to see all of* **Fehinti**, *standing on soil in the empty space of the theatre stage.*

The moment when our relationship with living things became one-sided and without exchange.

We profit, forget and move on.
We profit, forget and move on.

SECTION 24: Climate genocide, or what 1.5 and 2 degrees means in Africa

Past European empires have had a direct effect on this temperature increase, through their exploitation of lands and people. Now, European Ministers and the United Nations have signed a death warrant for those same people, by setting the target of stopping global warming at 2 degrees . . . with an aim of stopping at 1.5.

But here's what that looks like . . .

A projection of a map of Africa appears behind **Fehinti**.

In West Africa (again where I have inherited all my sauce from) and parts of North Africa, the seasons are unlike here. They have the wet season and the dry season. In the wet season, you plant your crop and in the dry season, you reap your crop. Now, at 1.5 degrees increase, drought is extended in all parts of Africa.

But if we zoom in on West Africa, this is what we see.

Animated map zooms into West Africa.

In West Africa the drought is extended by six months, that's half the year. Imagine the effect on food and crops.

Then, at 2 degrees increase in temperature, that goes up to nine months' worth of drought.

And at 3 degrees increase, West Africa experiences two years' worth of drought.

And this isn't the worst area affected in Africa, no, that's North Africa . . .

The map moves to North Africa.

Because, North Africa has seven months' worth of drought at 1.5 degrees. Twenty months' worth of drought at 2 degrees. And then, at 3 degrees, North Africa experiences five years' worth of drought.

We are talking about climate genocide.

SECTION 25: Ken moment 2 – Who are you serving?

Change of lighting. A flash of light at back of view represents a car. A sound and flash represent police. We are again somewhere else, in almost darkness.

Ken Where are we going?

Police (*V/O*) Don't worry, when we get there, you'll know.

Ken Why do/ ?

Police (*V/O*) Don't worry. At least you know you're in the safe hands of the police.

Ken The Ogoni people have settled in this area as farmers and fisherman since remembered time. Before the British colonialists invaded them in 1901. Within thirteen years, they had destroyed the fabric of Ogoni society.

So, my question to you, suh, is to whose hands do you refer, in which I am safe?

Because it seems both the hands and body with which you implement protection, do not belong to you, nor work for yours or our benefit.

Engine rumbles. The vehicle begins moving.

Silence.

Lighting change. Back in the studio space.

SECTION 26: Deji's realisation – The system is rigged

We see the crew working and resetting for the next moment.

Deji Yo, Fey. Look, I've had a thought.

Fehinti Yeah, man?

Deji So I'm sat there thinking about how my dad, right, he came to this country to get a career, earn money and send it home. Standard, you know?

Fehinti Yeah, man.

Deji But now I'm deepin it coz part of what he's doing is sending money to rebuild homes hit by storms, or for food that's not even growing properly.

Fehinti Yeah, man.

Deji It's not even for the nice stuff. I mean it's for survival but like a very different kind of survival right?

Fehinti Yeah man

Deji So what ? – my dad's no activist, bro . . . but if he's sending money . . . maybe he is? I dunno, fuck man.

Fehinti Yeaaaaah, man.

SECTION 27: Carbon sinks

Deji *stands thinking about this, watching* **Fehinti** *get into position.* **Fehinti** *seeing* **Kwami***, takes him into account.* **Fehinti** *is in a circle on the floor. Projections of water and trees fill the circle.* **Fehinti** *speaks to camera.*

Look, this big beautiful planet is powerful, and has been here for a long time. See, it takes what's in the air and makes use of it. Carbon sinks.

Carbon sinks store and reduce the amount of carbon in the atmosphere, reducing the earth's natural warming.

The two main stores are our oceans and our forests. Our oceans store about a quarter of all the carbon we have in our air.

With plankton and coral reefs absorbing carbon and converting CO_2 into food and using it for growth.

At foot level coral grows. **Fehinti***'s voice becomes a voiceover, and he stops talking and listens, observing the fish and coral. He is being eased by the earth's natural healing.*

However, because the ocean is getting hotter, it can't store as much carbon, like how a fizzy drink goes flat when it's hot.

And this is making it more acidic. Which is killing off coral reefs and plankton. Which means it absorbs even less carbon.

The coral dies.

This is what is called, ironically, a positive feedback loop.
Going round in circles until it can loop no longer.

The channel changes – screen blacks out.

SECTION 28 – What are the government doing? / Rap battle

Fehinti *is a politician in a TV studio on a politics panel show, a backdrop of Westminster behind him, wearing a suit. The beat is full of trumpets and trap drops.*

Government MP We cannot be complacent about this. Yes we've reduced emissions 23 per cent since 2010, 42 per cent since 1990, whilst the economy has doubled in size. You know we're doing a lot here, including the target that by 2050 we'll reduce all our greenhouse emissions by 80 per cent.

Music starts – we see that **Fehinti***, dressed as* **Fehinti***, is also on the panel programme.*

Fehinti Sorry, sorry, you said 42 per cent, yeah?

Government MP Yes.

Fehinti Are you sure?

Government MP Yes, I do believe that /

Fehinti Coz 42 per cent does not include the emissions that are going up.

Government MP Well . . .

Fehinti Aviation and shipping emissions are going up.

Government MP Hold on!

Fehinti Importing goods – you're not showing us.
Exporting goods – you're not showing us.

Government MP OK!

Fehinti The targets you set for the future,
You drop like a pin,
But we're not set to reach it.
Are you goading us?

Government MP Well, well, I'm loving your energy, love what you do.
Look you care for the planet.
And that's good for you.
The figures you talk about are so itty bitty bitty,
It's making you look a bit silly.
The target's for 2050, that's the reason we're keeping our millions.

Fehinti Reports of the truth ain't the truth for most for us.

Government MP The truth is a thing that I consider torturous.
The thing that you think is the truth for now, changes.
The future is brought to us.

Fehinti You don't really care and you're showing us.
Remember your actions with Covid, your targets, your hubris.
This is what you do to us.

Government MP Pandemic was new for us.
Your outlook is ludicrous.
One man with facts
You cannot move to us.
I'll take your version of history
Lock it within the ministry
And talk about the dynasty
Like Julius

Fehinti Caesar?
What?
Hold on.
What happened to saying you'll do a thing and then you do it?
What happened to laws protecting people moving through it?

We never had laws protecting people moving through it.
We only protect the money given when you do it.

Of the twenty-one indicators that we have for your targets, we only met four.
Of the thirty-one milestones we need for 2050, we only met two,
and I realise . . .

Government MP There's some incomplete . . .

Fehinti But I'm smelling defeat, when you barely compete.
You tell me . . .

Government MP The work's being done!

Fehinti And I tell you it's gas and you're talking for fun.
Imma tell you like 9.8 billion
Invested in fossil fuels
In just one year.
9.8 billion
In fossil fuels.

I'm smelling emissions!
Emissions, Emissions
Emissions, Emissions, Emissions, Emissions (x2)

I'm talking 'bout living conditions
I'm talking, Emissions

Emissions, Emissions
Emissions, Emissions, Emissions, Emissions (x2)

I'm talking 'bout living conditions
I'm talking Emissions, Emissions,
Emissions, Emissions.

So what you saying bro? for the whole of us.
Cos your failures are present and they are monstrous.
What guarantees do you actually have for the future?

Government MP You know, there's a lot that's being done.

Fehinti Not the things that you say to placate the masses,
But inaction, it's actually not the one.

Like you realise that 2 degrees, that's my nan's house being flooded,
A reaction that's not the one.
I smell Emissions.

Emissions, Emissions
Emissions, Emissions, Emissions, Emissions

I'm talking 'bout living conditions
I'm talking Emissions, Emissions,
Emissions, Emissions. (x2)

Government MP   Hold on hold on! If I could just get a word in here. We are world leaders in dropping Emissions, Emissions.

Fehinti   Emissions aren't changing enough.

Government MP   Tell that to the rest of the world. What about China? Surely their Emissions, Emissions, Emissions, Emissions are higher?

Your irritation, however vigorous, does not serve your desire, or change the fact that Britain leads.

We pan out showing a TV playing the politics programme, on a table in the studio. **Fehinti** *stands next to the TV.*

Fehinti *addresses us to camera.*

Britain leads?

Silence – click: the TV turns off.

Britain outsources its goods, their emissions are ours.
Yes, we're doing our part,
Shipping to here from afar.
Shipping from there, here we are.
Avoidance – a beautiful art.
Shame it is leaving some scars.
Please just look where we are.
The planet is falling apart.
The planet is falling apart.
The planet is falling apart.

Do you really think you are doing your part, Mr Government?

Tribal heavy breathing is heard in the background. Claps build to be many many hands, none of which we see, but we hear and feel their mass.

With your considering new oil fields,
With your HS2,
What does it really do?

Clap.

How much did you destroy,
with your Heathrow runway expansion?

Clap.

With your shipping off recycling to 'developing' countries?

Clap.

With your offshore investment in fossil fuels?

Clap.

With your not subsidising renewable energy research?
With your subsidising fossil fuels?

Clap.

With your subsidising fossil fuels?
With your subsidising fossil fuels?

Fehinti *is about to scream, whole. Primal. A close up on* **Fehinti**'s *face cuts to –*

SECTION 29: THE MAN DEM – How to get shit done

We now pan out and see all the faces we met in the beginning, **Deji***, the band,* **Dickson***, etc., each talking over each other at a large wooden table in the middle of the empty space. It's heated and the energy is high.*

Deji So it's bait as fuck. It's just like gun control in America, (*everyone hums in agreement*), everyone knows, but no one's budging, coz it's a money ting.

Kwami Bro, it's with the biggest – I got to turn my phone off for this one yeah. Coz you now how they get you. But the stuff that really tends to get shit DONE, ALWAYS tends to be a violent ting you get me . . .

Everyone laughs.

Fehinti OK, I hear that, but historically . . .

Deji Listen, yes, we recycle, we do our little bits.

Fehinti No, it's not about fucking recycling, bro, come on!

Kwami We're not disagreeing with you, bro.

Fehinti No, no, no. We put pressure on our government, and they push to take away our right to protest and give more powers to the police.

Kwami Listen, bro . . .

SECTION 30: Burn the table (continuous)

Fehinti Look, I am four times more likely to have force used against me if I am arrested than my white counterpart.

We are eight more likely to be stopped and searched.

It's not about safety, it's about silence.

Kwami Bro, we're not like you – you're clearly much further along than we are . . .

Fehinti No, I'm not. I'm really not.

Kwami Listen to me, bro. Coz at the end of day all I know how to do is survive. Yeah?

Everyone hmmms in agreement.

Kwami I wanna recycle, bro I do, I already do, but at the end of the day, I just wanna work, get some p's, get a seat at the table.

Deji Thank you. We're all just trying to get a seat at the table. That's it.

Fehinti A seat at the table?

That table was built off the backs and resources of our ancestors, for which they were raped and pillaged. No, that table is the reason you have to fight just to have the basics. Bruv, it screws you then makes you think everything is your fault.

Reduce, reuse, recycle, that's it right? Right?

But the only one that really caught on was the recycle bit, why? Because it tells you, you don't have to do very much.

Because I did my bit, I recycled.

Instead of the 100 companies that are responsible for 70 per cent of the world's emissions changing anything. Really.

Deji Yeah, but what am I meant to do?

Fehinti This system, this system makes you feel guilty for not being able to afford the eco version of something when you have literal government corruption funding oil companies.

How does that make sense? What, coz Big Daddy Capitalism says get money and fuck whatever else?

Bro, racism, sexism, ableism, climate change, they're all just symptoms of the same disease. A disease that's making a very small amount of people a lot of fucking money.

You get it? Coz you think it's just you. Or that house down the road, and that systems of power don't need challenging, don't need changing.

That table is the table that tells you that you have no power. I don't want a seat at the fucking table.

Deji Yo, Faints, calm down.

Fehinti Don't, don't tell me to calm down! Shit, man, sorry. I don't want to be quiet to make you feel comfortable. I'm not calm! I'm not fucking OK!

I don't want a seat at the table, I want to burn it!

The table they are sitting around bursts into flames.

SECTION 31: Ken 3 – our futures ripped away

Change of lighting. Police lights. Darkness, bar the light of a car behind and in front of **Fehinti**. *Bumpy-terrain and engine sounds in the background.*

Ken   The once beautiful Ogoni countryside is no longer a source of fresh air and green vegetables. All one sees and feels around is death. And I am to understand that, worldwide, we are not the only ones having our futures ripped from the bosom of our descendants.

> I write as Ken Saro-Wiwa, the man.
> Once I leave this car I know what I will enter.
> For the progress we have made. The demonstrates that they laughed at but now they fear.
> And to that I say, Lord take my soul, but the struggle continues.

Off camera.

Mum   Fehinti?

Mum   Fehinti?

SECTION 32: Mum

Fehinti *turns and walks back into the living room set where he began. His* **Mum** *is sitting on the sofa. He joins her. It is the only lit space in the darkness of the empty stage.*

Fehinti   Hi.

Mum   Hi. My living room is nicer than this.

Fehinti   Mum, what are you doing here?

Mum   You were not answering my calls or replying to my texts.

Fehinti   I'm doing my environmental project, I told you this.

Mum   Busy recruiting people?

Fehinti   I'm not recruiting people, I'm . . . what are you supposed to do when the government makes protest illegal?
You know about Ken Saro-Wiwa, right?

Mum   I know him, of course I do.

Fehinti   Yeah, OK, so I didn't. I had to Google to find out about him. I didn't know anything about that movement. I didn't know he led the biggest climate movement in the world, hundreds and thousands of people of colour. I didn't know anything about it.

Mum   Did he do it by himself?

Fehinti   No, he didn't do it by himself. It was him and the Ogoni Nine, other initiatives, but it worked. It really worked. Shell left.

Mum   It worked, he was executed. Fehinti . . .

Fehinti   I know.

Mum   He was executed.

Fehinti   I know. God. I'm angry.

Mum   Angry at me?

Fehinti   No, not at you. I don't want to sacrifice myself, I'm not a martyr. I'm nothing like that, I just . . . I am so angry at all the people that have had to die for them to care, that people sacrificed their own lives. I'm angry at governments that make me feel small. I'm angry at whole situations that make me feel powerless. I don't want to sacrifice myself. I just want people to be as angry as I am, and then do something.

Mum   I am more aware of the issues. I have become more educated about the environmental problem, but you see, people like you, people like me, they're not going to sacrifice themselves. They are not going to put themselves in the forefront, not for this cause. They have their own issues. They've got children to bring up, they've got to put food on the table. Some people are jobless, some people are homeless, some people are hopeless.

Some are waiting for the papers to come from the Home Office.

And you expect them to put themselves on the forefront? That's not going to happen. They are not going to do that. I am not going to do that.

SECTION 33: Kiss me hold me

The camera looks at them sitting with a distance between them, saying nothing. **Fehinti** *looks out, talking to the space.* **Mum** *is also silently looking forward. It's moving in almost slow motion.*

Music.

> I was hoping
> Wasn't living
> Coulda give in
> Wasn't winning
> I just need to be held
>
> I just want to be held (x2)
>
> See I was looking
> I was finding
> Heat is climbing

Didn't give in
But I just need to be held

I just need to be held (x2)

Kiss me, hold me, watch me weep
Kiss me, hold me, watch me weep
Kiss me, hold me, watch me weep
I need you to just
Kiss me, hold me, watch me weep
I need you to just

I want you to just
Kiss me
Hold me
Watch me weep

I appreciate
The work you've done for me
I know, I know it wasn't easy
I hear

Your pain and regret
Your frustrations are clear,

Just descended from fear

I know
It hits you
Right. Here. (x4)

Kiss me hold me watch me weep
I want you to just
Kiss me hold me watch me weep
I need you to just
Kiss me hold me watch me weep
I need you to just

I want you to just
Kiss me
Hold me
Watch me weep

Hoooooo
Hooooo
(*Build.*)

Fehinti *stands and walks back into the studio, walking past the* **Mandem** *in heated debate. Trying to get their attention.*

> Hold me and I'll hold you back
> Can't keep eye contact
> My have panic attack
> Climate anxiety and that
> Finding it hard to relax
> Don't mean to back track
>
> Because I'm British and but I'm other
> The lines that separate each other
> If you have a need, people say it was
> Me that stole it brother
> It wasn't me that stole it brother
> It wasn't we that stole it brother
> The people are stealing
> Pitting us
> against each other
>
> I know
> It hits you
> Right. Here. (x4)
>
> Kiss me hold me watch me weep
> I want you to just
> Kiss me hold me watch me weep
> I need you to just
> Kiss me hold me watch me weep
> I need you to just
>
> I want you to just
> Kiss me
> Hold me
> Watch me weep

SECTION 34: What are we supposed to do?

The **Mandem** *are now surrounding* **Fehinti**. **Mum** *comes out of the room, and* **Grandma** *joins the group.*

Deji   It's easy to feel overwhelmed, so what do you want us to do?

Tee   I don't know what you want from me bro.

Dickson   What would you like us to do, bro?

Chloe   What shall we do?

Mum   What do you want us to do, Fehinti?

Grandma   What can I do, my son?

SECTION 35: Ken's advice

A projection of Ken Saro-Wiwa appears behind **Fehinti**.

Ken Saro-Wiwa, the Ogni Nine, the Bill of Rights for Indigenous People. For the hundreds of actions that you see, there are tens of thousands of actions that go unseen.

It's not about the individual. Yeah, that might be how you start, but it can't be how we make change. We've got to group together as a collective, because if we saw, if we knew how much we had achieved . . . what we need to achieve wouldn't seem so extreme.

The iron shutters open behind **Fehinti** *and reveal activists of colour filling auditorium.* **Fehinti** *turns towards them and is filmed facing out into the auditorium as the music builds and builds.*

SECTION 36: Fehinti is not alone. Gallery of heroes

Fehinti *walks out into the auditorium, turns and sits on the steps surrounded by people. Choral music plays underneath all of this section: 'Yeah, yeah, yeah'. It's beautiful and fills the space with life. There are a few moments of just the music, before any speaking.*

Fehinti   I often get asked: what's the solution, how do we fix it? I don't know, but I do know we're not starting from the beginning. There are people that have done and continue to do this work.

Camera pans up from **Fehinti** *and travels to an audience member who stands and speaks to the camera. This audience member is a community hero; an activist. Each hero introduces themselves and what they do. Five activists, people of the Global Majority, introduce themselves in turn, describing the work they do and their activism.*

'Yeah, yeah, yeah' plays in full blast as we just stop and watch them talk.

Samia   Hi my name is Samia. I'm twenty-five years old, born and raised in East London. I started *Seize the Vote* with my friends because we felt that we had no access to good education. We started *Seize the Vote* to empower young people of colour, so they could access political power.

Nick   Hi my name is Nick Amin. I'm part of the *Transition Movement*, part of *Extinction Rebellion*, part of *Stand Up To Racism*, and quite a few other movements. Now, what all these movements are trying to do is to fight for justice, because they realise, we all realise, that injustice anywhere is a threat to Justice everywhere. And, in that respect, we're all tied together in a single government of destiny, fighting for justice.

Helen My name is Helen and I organise for *Border Abolition*. In 2017 I was part of an action that stopped the deportation charter flight to Nigeria and Ghana. We did this because we believe in undoing borders, and we recognise that these flights are part of a long and violent history, which denies people their fundamental rights to home, to safety, and to care.

Joshua My name is Joshua Virasami. I'm thirty years old and I'm a charity worker. I'm also a member of the *London Renters Union*, a climate collective called *Wretched of the Earth*, and *Black Lives Matter* UK. I was born and raised in Hounslow, West London, and my family came here from Mauritius, where most of them still reside. But, wherever my people live, we know we live in a divided world. A world of the dividers – the rich and powerful; and the divided – the disempowered. A world of theft, and a world of violence. I organise in the tradition of Fred Hampton, of Leila Khaled, a tradition of Revolution, a tradition that says we need change root-and-branch. From Kashmir to the Congo, from Palestine to right here. A tradition that teaches us that the people united can never be defeated.

Sarah I'm Sarah from *Women of Colour* in the *Global Women's Strike*. We campaign for a 'care income' for everybody who cares for people and defends the planet. Beginning with mothers, who work the hardest, and starting with the global South, where women are bearing all the survival work and keeping people alive. I'm African-American, I'm an immigrant and I know how hard my grandmother worked as a farmer. All of those connections brought me to this movement – and this movement is much bigger than we think. Right now farmers in India are in a massive strike, people all over the world are fighting for food, for justice against racism. And those movements are all one. We're not starting from scratch, there are many of us. We are here in our millions, and we're demanding the resources so that we can thrive and rebuild our communities.

SECTION 37: Art and activism (continuous)

The camera comes back to **Fehinti**. *He is sitting on the stairs in the auditorium, in-between the seats. He is talking to the audience, and to us, the camera.*

Fehinti You lot are so piff! It's mad. And really inspiring and thank you for being here.
  Look, I got together with an amazing group of people and we created this.
  I didn't want to make this originally,
  I just wanted to fly around the world, win my Oscar, release my mixtape – again, not a joke.

SECTION 38: Fehinti's truth / Can I Live?

Music starts. **Fehinti** *stands and, as he speaks, he moves back onto the stage.*

  I'm . . .

I'm new to this
but my presence is necessary.

I came clean cut with clarity
coz it's all looking pretty hairy.

And I'm intolerant to the lies
So I'm reducing all my diary.

No, I'm not a vegan but the situation is scary.
So I stopped eating meat 'n fish and, clearly . . .

I moved on to a different way of thinking, sincerely,
Took on all the actions adhering to that theory
To recycle, not fly, buy clothes bi-yearly.

Clearly, there's more if these politicians are going to hear me.
For real.

Music fully starts, **Fehinti** *performs with the band.* **Dickson** *and* **Deji** *dance with him.*

Deep contemplation and irritation
The reasons, they are adjacent.
The reasons for speculation,
It's true that things are changing.

What's more it's moving crazy.

I get it, I feel my nation
I get it, I feel my nation
The problems are dominating.

To think about climate change when
When rent needs over paying.

Division, it comes with hatred
'n fear is so suffocating.

I get it I feel my nation
I get it I feel my nation
I get I feel my nation.

They're feeling, can I live?

If you're feeling irrelevant
Let me remind you you're heaven sent
Duplicitous world
Felling malevolent

So stride with the elegance
Come looking definite
Know that your place in this world is important
Intelligent
Yes, you're intelligent
Don't be tricked to believe you're irrelevant
Boy, it's relevant
So be diligent
Show love to my immigrants
In crisis you're killin' it
Pandemics they came
And your value was limitless
Look, we're marking the differences.

I wouldn't be here if it weren't for them
They add to our wealth, is it worse for them?

Can they live?

Can I live though?
Can I live?
Can I live though?
Just wanna live, can I live?
Can I live?
Can I live though?

Everyone who has worked on the show from crew to directors and producers is now on the stage dancing. The camera cuts between the audience dancing and **Fehinti** *performing onstage. It is now a concert.*

Working class revolution
Yes, we can learn for them

Hard working people
Need a future that we can earn for them

It's so simple,
our knowledge just needs some servicing

Individual action is a term that needs repurposing

I'm new to the game
But your presence is necessary

Came clean cut with the bars
Coz it's all looking pretty hairy

I'm intolerant to the lies
And I'm reducing all my dairy

No, I'm not a vegan but the situation is scary

So I stopped eating meat 'n fish and clearly
I moved on to a different way of thinking, sincerely.

Like when you realise you're hooked
And you stop bingeing or drinking or thinking about anything else but sinking.

Can I live?
Can I live though?
Can I live though?

Credits.

END

I Am Sending You the Sacred Face

Heather Christian

A lip-synch drag piece about Mother Teresa. In this musical act Mother Teresa is riddled with self-doubt about her life's work. She wrestles with her own fame, faith and legacy. In this piece a man plays a woman, a saint and flawed human, the public mask and the inner person/soul. This text is written in a unique cadence, playing with the sound of and musicality of words themselves, and interplay of various linguistic registers.

This piece premiered on 14 December, 2020 on Theater in Quarantine's channel on YouTube.

Theater in Quarantine began creating and streaming work online in March 2020 from the closet of the East Village apartment of Joshua William Gelb. The closet measures 4 foot by 8 foot by 2 foot.

Heather Christian is a US singer, performer, playwright, and composer originally from New Orleans, Louisiana. Her works include *Animal Wisdom* (2017), and *Oratorio for Living Things*, which ran Off-Broadway at Ars Nova in spring of 2022, after being interrupted in 2020. She premiered the music-theatre piece *Terce* in 2024 and is the composer of the musical *A Wrinkle in Time,* based on the novel by Madeline L'Engle, which premieres at Arena Stage in Washington DC in 2025.

From the Author: How *I Am Sending You the Sacred Face* came to be

A Little Context

On 13 March, 2020, I walked out of a theatre at 4pm in state of non-reality after having cancelled the world premiere run of my music-theatre piece *Oratorio for Living Things* two previews in due to Covid-19, a global pandemic no one understood or knew how to stop. At 4.30 pm, I took a train home to the Hudson Valley, counted how many toilet paper rolls and boxes of pasta we had, and started the exceptionally lengthy process of trying to hold my own hand through a terrifying event that I could do absolutely nothing about. We were all there, so I'll be brief. Of course, there was fear and grief, there was rest, there was boredom, there was outrage – a full gamut of feelings and experiences happened between the four walls of our homes and apartments those two years, which we are still purging or processing. I mention all this because I think it's important to know that *this* is the strange once-in-a-lifetime protoplasm that grew *I Am Sending You the Sacred Face*. The surreal mix of despair and boredom and unknowing turned me away from all the shows I had been writing up to that point and instead, turned me to Facebook (of all places) where I got updates from one particularly unsinkable friend of mine (and his partner in co-creation) who had turned his closet into a theatre and was programming a season's worth of shows, hell, highwater or plague.

I'm talking about Joshua William Gelb and Katie Rose McLaughlin of Theater in Quarantine in New York City, who I have dubbed the Patron Saints of Post-Covid theatre recovery. They single handedly saved the flailing spirits of theatre lovers and reminded us of who we are at our best and at our cores: curious and deep thinkers with insatiable appetites for beauty and humour. Just because there wasn't a stage didn't mean there wasn't a theatre. It was thrilling. Anyways, at some point they were taking suggestions via social media for what musicals they should attempt, and being a bit of a squeaky wheel –
I cold-called them.
'You should just let me write something spec for you.'
'Do you have any ideas?' –

It is also important for you to know that at the time, I had a file folder on my computer labelled 'Maybe Bad Ideas' which included many questionable unwritten shows, including 'Mother Teresa: The Musical.' I had a Zoom with Josh and Katie Rose, read the full list of clunkers to them over coffee and this is the one they picked.

This all seems very off-hand and glib, but I swear to you, it was a decision on a whim, initially. It was a torch in my heart that got sparked from a very unlikely question, which is 'why the hell not?' I usually never make work on so tepid a beach. I am usually of the mind that if it is not essential somehow, that I should not make it. This is just my personal cross to bear. But at the time, I had no clue where my creative compass was pointed or what was essential. The slate had not only been wiped clean, it had also been thrown against the wall and blown to smithereens. All I knew was that I missed people. I missed people and the alchemical healing of making art with people. I missed people so desperately much, which was a huge surprise to me, as I consider myself downright monastic.

'Mother Teresa: The Musical', at the time, did not exist. I'd never written a musical top to tail in a couple of months. What I knew was: I was making something for Theater in Quarantine to be performed by Josh in his closet, it was about Mother Teresa in some way, it was for an audience of one person in their homes hopefully wearing stereo headphones, it was not to exceed an hour in length. Given all those things, I decided that what this meant is that I'd be writing/recording/producing a musical theatre concept album of sorts that would have to then be turned into a grand lip synch.

On Mother Teresa Herself

What was beautiful about lockdown was that I could spend all day immersed in research without interruption. No one needed my attention. I read everything Mother Teresa published in her lifetime as well as three biographies – but I really *found* the show when I stumbled upon her collected letters which were published posthumously and, from what can be inferred from her character and life, *without* her consent. It was through these letters that I became privy to the dark night of the soul that she endured secretly for over fifty years, which is, according to theologians, the longest dark night on record.

A 'dark night of the soul' is a term coined by Saint John of the Cross, and it refers to a period of holy living wherein the devotee (usually someone living an ascetic practice) feels 'abandoned' by God and whose life's purpose is therefore thrown into question. Dark Nights are sometimes followed by ecstatic reunions with God and one's purpose – but sometimes, a Dark Night isn't followed by anything but inevitable death and sometimes, canonization. The lives of the saints are usually told by others centuries after the fact and have been tidied up to accommodate happy conclusions which breathe meaning into what otherwise read as lives filled with often pointless and always consistent suffering. The lives of the saints are macabre, and religious ecstasy is slippery. It is not rare to read of a Dark Night, but it is exceedingly rare to read a first-hand account of one happening in the modern world. Mother Teresa's letters are heartbreaking proof of the duplicitous nature of her 'faces' and why they were necessary for living in this newly globalized world: A world so obsessed with visibility and comfortable in its cognitive dissonance that it can both celebrate her repeated insistence to 'not be seen' and simultaneously laser print her smiling face on a 15-Euro Vatican gift shop T-shirt. Here is where I found the essential (to me) thing to write: Living through a pandemic is to endure / enjoy invisibility, to endure/ enjoy a Dark Night, to endure/ enjoy duplicity. If there was a patron saint of invisibility, of dark nights, of showing one face to protect the sanctity of the other – Mother Teresa is it.

Production

I knew from the beginning that I wanted to make this piece in triptych, structurally – three 'panels', each containing an aspect of the saint. One panel (or in my case, musical movement) contains the face we all know – the outfit, the point of view, the image on the candles and the T-shirts: I called this panel the 'Sacred Face.' The second panel (movement) is the internal life and soul, which Mother Teresa herself refers to as 'an empty room.' She is actively trying to empty herself of everything but the space where God could occupy if He ever returns. She must 'keep this room clean' which means obliterating any trace of pride in her accomplishments or, paradoxically, in her humility.

It includes obliterating any trace of her desires including her faith itself. She articulates that reading the 'Stabbat Mater' brings her much consolation, so it seemed fitting to call this panel the 'Sacred Heart.' And then of course there is the third panel which is a panel that I am abstract painting cheekily with joyful abandon, filled with wild speculation about what it is that Mother Teresa could impart to *us*, right now, as we are all, un-saintly and unholy, being thrust upon our own Dark Nights. I flatter myself (now that she's dead) that she'd want to talk to us. I flatter myself (now that she's osmosed into the cloud where all spirits return, maybe) that she'd want to help. This third panel is the 'Sacred Now.'

This is a performance in drag. I have been truly fortunate to have been able to sing with/ make work with some of the most incredible artists working in the sphere of Drag Performance that this world has ever seen (Taylor Mac, Salty Brine, Martha Graham Cracker, Kimberly Clark, Tigger-James Ferguson, Machine Dazzle to name just a few). These extraordinary artists have schooled, nurtured, included me. I consider drag to be one of the highest arts, one of physical and spiritual alchemy. As an intimate outsider, it has always struck me that perhaps one of the most useful and brilliant aspects of drag performance is that within it, you can invent a 'face' fabulous and powerful enough to be ABOVE all of the cynicism and cruelty of this world and wear this fabulous face like an armour to absorb the arrows, keeping the soft underbelly of the human who has maybe endured quite enough of it in their lives intact. A gorgeous walnut in a gorgeous shell. Mother Teresa insists that the outer persona (her 'shell') must appear to be joyful and radiant enough to distract the onlooking world from the vulnerable shrinking person under her cloak. There is a beautiful grey area where Mother Teresa and drag culture overlap, and I wanted to revel in this grey area with both levity and grace (and both reverence and irreverence for all things.) Because I'm not a drag artist myself, I hired a friend and artist I both love and admire, Dito Van Reigersburg aka Martha Graham Cracker to be our Drag Dramaturge – a position I invented for the explicit purpose of keeping us to that task.

Finally

I have often felt pressure from the outside world to hurry up and process the catastrophe of current moments and make something useful before the next catastrophe arrives. I have felt like 'art' is supposed to 'make sense' of a world that is actively burning – and with that perspective, it seems impossible. But what I can say is that I made *I Am Sending You the Sacred Face* with a singular delight and abandon born out of a will to find present tense meaning and not just retrospective sense. I tell you with delight that I stayed up all night for the first time in years, hot gluing sequins on to phones and laughing in a zoom room with collaborators who were making dinners, decorating Christmas trees, wiping down groceries while 'tech' was in process. I can tell you I felt nine years old, like anything was possible, like no one was paying attention, like I was free to think the full weird unacceptable and untidy thought and bust my guts laughing about it with friends. 'Why not throw the triptych into physical space?' 'Why not animate the mouths of the three Popes Pius so that they are singing the lyrics?' 'Why not use that ring light as a halo?' 'Why not make your costume out of your bedsheets and painters' tape?' 'Why not flashing hot pink neon? Marigold garlands? Slapstick?

Ikettes choreography?' The resounding 'why nots' that made the piece what it was could only have happened in a time and space as bizarre as the one we were living through. I think about that time now as the holding room for our spirits, and I'm so delighted that our spirits didn't want to sink under the weight of it all or disappear entirely – though some of that certainly occurred to us – but rather that our spirits wanted to sing, wanted to play.

Heather Christian

I Am Sending You the Sacred Face

One brief musical act with Mother Teresa
An expressionist drag performance in Triptch

The piece was written, composed and recorded by Heather Christian.
Directed and performed by Joshua William Gelb.
Produced by Theater in Quarantine & Theater Mitu's Expansion Works.

Music	**Heather Christian**
Choreography	**Katie Rose McLaughlin**
Drag dramaturgy	**Dito van Reigersberg**
Scenography	**Kristen Robinson**
Video Design	**Stivo Arnoczy**
Sound Design and Mix	**Ada Westfall**

ONE: Face

1. Poverty Talk

Desires are mosquitoes, not bites
That sari you want will also cost you bracelets
Somewhere we're taught we lose ourselves when we lose the things we like
then we repeated it until we proved 'em right
Nihil habentes et omnia possidentes

So I only speak for me as I am in the world, not of it
to choose poverty, you love it for its clarity
I like my rotten bulgar, I delight in days of hunger
I like patching over my old two saris,
I wear shoes that do not fit me
Stink and sweat, refuse a fan, a phone, a TV
Praise my louse-y bed and head and hall and company –
To work on poverty, to me, you must be poor.
My commonality with those I serve gives dignity
An equal at their eye
they come to us to die
With the dignity of friendship and with an uncontested equal

Nihil habentes et omnia possidentes
Nihil habentes et omnia possidentes

You say 'the poor' like they're one thing
like they're a theory and herd and not a people that outnumber you
not individual lives with crazy stories, mums and uncles,
similar struggles, same intentions, different means.

How many people have you alchemized to numbers?
How many voices did you mute behind the comfort of your screen?

Poverty is not a plague
It was not sent by God
but engineered by human systems,
He won't fix it, that's your job.

Poverty's no plague
It was not nature who bestowed it
But our selfish crazed ambitions that both
bought the gun and worked to load it.
Poverty's no plague
It's not a thing that simply happened

It is ours. And every second that continues passing while you are not offering your hand – yes, your REAL HAND
is a waste of time.

And time is unforgiving, so time is not like God (they say).

Nihil habentes et omnia possidentes

The message of my life. That was it.
It would be rude and misleading of me not to start with that.
To do otherwise would be bad dramaturgy, as that is the message here painted on the outside of this vessel. Yes, vessel.
This is a well-made vessel custom-built to relay that message to you,
the reason you got it was not because I thought it but because I became it with theatrics.

'Be the change you wish to see in the world' is a kind of drag.
The outfit matters.

But just so we are clear, it was not posturing, I truly believe this message to be objectively true:
Poverty is an exhaulted state.
I treat the poor with dignity as befits this exaulted state.
From a religious perspective the poor are closer to wisdom,
I do not treat the poor with dignity out of pity or compassion
I treat them with dignity as an act of reverence.
the poor are not just equal to you. From a religious perspective,
they are better.

I was not born poor, I chose it, along with this outfit.
There is symbolism in the outfit, always. Some people call that marketing.
You remember me when you see this outfit, and what do you remember?
Me, the person? No. My dreams? You remember my dreams. This outfit affords me that kind of subliminal messaging. It's a teeny tiny phonecall to a surfing synapses in your brain. Hello! (*Makes the 'hang ten' sign.*)

There is additional symbolism in the outfit in the colours,
which I will ennumerate here:
Faith is the inner tunic and is a brillliant white, the brilliant white of the teeth,
of the smile. This is a white so brilliant it is supposed to put out the eyes of the intellect, which is fabulous.

Now over this white tunic of faith we put a blue trim, a blue coat of mail.
Blue is hope, by which one is defended, see?
And also liberated from the thing that it ultimately represents: The world. More on that later.

Blue hope is an armor and covers the whole body, top to tail, with no openings save for a little visor which allows the soul only to look heavenward and nowhere else. More on THAT later.

Now over the white and over the blue, as a finishing touch, one puts on the precious robe.

This is charity. This is what everybody sees, when they see you after being blinded by your smile.
This is what you drag down the street. This is both the drag and what is drag. Yes?

Let's talk about calls.

2. Telephone Ballet

(*A tiny ballet with a telephone. Text is primarily voiceover. Only* **bolded** *lines should be lip synched.*)

I experienced a call when I was quite a young girl. **My first call, that is,** which is the call to be a nun. This is an understated call. An intuition laced with a desire. Most nuns and monks you speak to will tell you something similar. Like a phone in your heart. **The phone's in your heart. With this kind of call. Yes?** (*Something physical and absurd to signify a heart phone.*)

The second call I received was different. This was a phone in my face. This was an actual voice IN my face that I received when I was TRULY not expecting it. **On a train.** A voice of someone who did not sound at all like anyone I'd ever met and was urgent. This was an urgent phonecall from inside my face, that I received while riding a train, and THIS was the call that got us here tonight,

me from
wherever the heck I am and you from –
wherever the heck you are
somehow serendipitously

in the same place.

3. The Call

(*Train whistle.*)

FACE   the VOICE
this is where it started: He said –

                                       (*Your heart was never drowned in sorrow as my mother's*)

I said: I stand with the mother
I dress as your mother dressed and perform her always, he said:

(Will you not show me)

I said: I will show you like this –
I stand with the mother, as the mother, alright? always
I promised him as such, that promise is a cup that I fill
with my work and love and minutes.

(Go now to the poor)

This conversation frightened me

(Go now to the poor)

God was testy, this is what was hard to bear
God did not make requests of me, He dared.
And when I paused –

(Will you not?)

like a child who's been neglected, toward the dry arms of its father

(Won't you, go ahead and try me, will you not?)

Not will you? Not can you? Not may you?

(Will you not)

not 'won't you' but

(You probably will not)

I DID try to stop the thoughts.
I tried to be in silence.
I could not, it came on booming
in a train car to Darjeeling

(Will you not?)

then every morning after as a panic in my memory

(Go, go now, go now, go quickly, will you not?)

What is asked is just as natural as it is supernatural

I Am Sending You the Sacred Face

the voice lives in two places at once –
in the train car at 80 miles an hour, impossible
and in the traveling space between the drums of my ears
as love made ghost, made clear, and argumentative.

(Go now to the poor, why do you not?)

I say my answer lies with priests who know much better

(Then you won't?)

Was this my first act of cowardice? I am too young at this point to decide.
Is obedience cowardice?

(Every day you do not leave passes in darkenss.
One hundred passed in agony today, will you not?)

Ultimately, the church would not consent til I could promise it success
but what is this success?
What is success in matters of the hopeless?

(What now?)

so 'Let me go' I said tormented 'Success is just a silly word that you invented.'
My doubt lived as an oily film on the well of my conviction
deep enough to where no skiv could drop an anchor
My doubt floats at the top, but all the same pollutes the water.

(Forgo caution, child, will you not?)

When God asks for things, people are careful about details
when society asks for things, they are done quickly.

(Hurry hurry hurry
Forgo caution, child, will you not?)

This thirst is infinite
This is a thirst that I rushed to put out like a trillion fires in a thousand
    neighbourhoods,
I can't find them all in time
Quenching won't be possible.

(Don't let that ease your mind!
Just because it is untennable does not mean that it's not your calling
Will you NOW?)

ok

                                                                          now

ok

                                                                          now

ok

                                                                          now

ok

                                                                          now

in the beginning you are vain.

God has spoken to you through a telephone in your face.
But a soul canoe don't float
A soul canoe don't float
if you want divine perspective you have to get up out the boat.

Don't you strain at your brother's gnat
and swallow your own camel
Don't you claim that your brother's whack
with a soul that's still a gamble.

You will know you're a beginner if your rapture is a show
If it's public and you're pleased now to let everybody know
So a dark night's to be suffered
not to punish you, but bolster
both your real legs to the parapet –
If a beginners on a pride trapeeze God will
vamoose the net.

There is competition even in virtue. I will not hide from you that I have my share of wanting to be the best at something. I was proud of my humility. In the beginning. Are you? I ask that without an agenda, as we are two songs in now and so – we are officially friends. (*Big smile*.)

'Be the change you wish to see in the world' is a kind of drag – I already said that.

4. Wounding Ritual

What I wanted to see more of in the world was humility. So I became that change in order to fulfill my wish of seeing it. For most folks, humility is pretty unappealing – for one thing you only

get humility by acquiring humiliations. Nobody likes that.
Except for me.
I accept humiliations, I am grateful for them, I call them my sweetie sweets.

(*Big smile.*)

My smile is a cloak, not a coat
it doesn't keep me warm, but covered
it doesn't protect me, but you. It's part of the outfit, and furthermore doesn't interfere with humility.

I just wanted to be a nun, really. Ordered. Submissive. I never wanted to be the leader. Being a leader requires a certain level of belief in one's self, which is a whisper's breadth from pride – which is a different kind of cloak. One that protects ME and not YOU, and –
I wouldn't abandon anyone like that.

Abandonment is an awful poverty. Abandonment is what I call a second wound.

The first wound is a given, you will be wounded. In this life.
but the second wound is one that comes just after it and lasts a very long time
that second wound is a wound of 'no one was concerned I was wounded in the first place'.
I am telling you this so you can do your best
to make sure you aren't opening these second wounds – anymore.

Anyways, in the end I wasn't taught the reality of feeling unloved and unwanted by others, I was taught that by God.

But – patched clothes are no disgrace. It is the same with spirits.

Is loving your system the same thing as loving your breakfast? Don't answer that.

If you get the voice, you get it once
the voice has other ports of entry after that
did you know girl, when you heard it,
it would never speak again?
that it would leave you ironed flat against its silence?

Being the change you wish to see in the world is kind of a drag.

5. Cataclysm

A shift into a 'different kind of show'.
Abrasive sound cue that wipes the slate in a sufficient (or catastrophic) way.
Bird calls, gunshots, implosions, lightning strikes, screaming, heavy rain, a deafening apocalype, a phone's empty dialtone –
Then five whole seconds of silence.

TWO: The Sacred Heart (of Darkness)

Cleaning the room of stuff.

6. I Am Empty

my soul is out of its onesie
isn't coddled. Is big enough to be put down, weaned.
Made to eat a bread with a crust. That is St. John's explanation for this silence.
And now my soul is exposed, it is ready.
prone to oxidation and a forceful gust of wind
and there are raptures, and transports,
a dislocation of the bones.

I annihilate myself, and strike this room of everything that was not part of the vessel,

I'm the manger, I'm the cup and I am ready,
I am empty I am empty I am empty I am empty I am empty I am empty I am empty

The living image of the saint is one of horror
of a mouth open and gaping at its own husk in the mirror
Surrounded by their own seeing
Spiders eviscerated in their own webs
Attacked by stronger giants
while they patch their robes with washrags or rub ashes into papercuts –

I annihilate myself, and strike this room of everything that was not part of the vessel,
I'm the manger, I'm the cup and I am ready,
I am empty I am empty I am empty I am empty I am empty I am empty I am empty

Cleaning the room of self.

7. The Idiot's Guide to Self Annihilation

Saints do not practice self care, we practice self annihiliation.
If I was to publish *The Idiot's Guide to Self Annihilation* it would be short,
and likely not your favourite book.
it would go like this:

Page One, first item:
Seek out some suffering, and then appreciate it when it shows up.
It is hard to explain this to a modern person, this want of suffering

You cannot look at it with what you call your right mind.
But, without suffering, the work we do is social work,
which is good and fine and helpful but
nothing to do with your soul, in my opinion.
anyway the work is not yours.

Page Two: this would be a blank page
followed by another blank page
and then there would be a page where I drew a single marigold.

I really like the reminder of a marigold. They are named for Mary, you know?
Who is the true example of watching and feeling and continuing to stand upright.
She blooms unseasonably.

(*A fly appears and becomes increasingly annoying.*)

Where am I?
Page Five, the second item:
Once you have located your suffereing, give a purpose to it. Give it to someone.
You got no one to suffer for? Alright, suffer for me.
Imagine that every time you lose your breath or you cry out in pain
that it is an offering in a lunch box of my energy
I collect it through the air, this is how I will go on,
because of you.

Your suffering has value.
Anyway the work is still not yours.
That's the whole book, guys.

I don't want to see my face. Anymore.
It's a thing I use, it's not a part of me, really.
I don't want your candles, I don't want your stuff
If its not abundantly clear, I am keeping this room vacant
in expectation of –

Well anyway He won't come in unless the room is spotless.

8. Phonecall Survey

Phone rings, a flip phone with 'ave Maria' ring tone.

Excuse me.

Mother Teresa answers it.

Hello?

I Am Sending You the Sacred Face

Inaudible   **MT**

~~Good morning and God bless you is this Mother Teresa~~

                                                Yes, I suppose it is.

~~This is a survey that is very official as to the nature of your progress within your calling, press one to comply~~

                                                (*She presses 'one'.*)

~~Welcome! Please answer the following questions with brutal honesty in order that we may fully assist you with your current station.~~
~~Question one:~~
~~Do I receive Holy Communion~~
~~with faith and love?~~

                                                No

~~Question three: Do I value the salvation of my soul?~~

                              I don't have one. There is nothing in me

~~Which are dangerous occasions of~~
~~mortal sin to which I am exposed?~~

                                                My eyes

~~are what~~

                                                Dangerous

~~because of the distraction from God~~

                                      Because of the dis – Exactly

~~Working …. thank you!~~
~~Do I desire to be poor with Christ's poor?~~

                                              With my whole heart
                 I am not humble but I am too small to be proud.
                        I pray fervently to be forgotten
                       to be ignored to be – nothing to anyone,
              and this is how my prayer has been answered.

(*Laughing.*)

> Why are you laughing.
> anyways I still keep on saying the same prayer.

~~Do I avoid 'trying to shine' in front of others?~~

> I don't understand the question.

~~Do I accept desolation as readily as consolation? Do I accept dryness in prayer as a grace of God?~~

> No nothing inside of me

~~Is there anything you'd like to add?~~

> Tell Him I'm sorry.
> ask Him to give me the face of a smiling child

~~Why is that my job~~

> Because He doesn't speak directly to me anymore.
> Hello? Hello?

(*Hangs up.*)

In a marriage some things are private. Kept even from the children
I cannot explain this part to you so why unload the cart.

9. Undefended

I am undefended. I live undefended. The only shield I've got now is my quiet.
and that isn't for myself
May my promise be a chalice,
I can pour into it lots of things like minutes
like sweat,

But not thoughts. 'Cause thoughts are of the self,
and I am emptying the cup of myself.

I am undefended. I live undefended. The only shield I've got now is my smile
but I don't give that to myself
Tell you, let's just see what happens when a modern woman
gives herself completely to be a blank space
will it keep her on her knees
to see what's emptied from the cup of herself?

A cup by nature won't track what it spills.
A cup has two states, filling and emptying.
I am in service. I have no actions of my own.

One might say I was purified of human alloy
One might say I was ready to enter the deep things of God
One might say I was terribly unkind to myself
One might say I was unable to look at the whole picture
One might say I was never able to understand whole picture
I have given myself to the small, to the one life at a time,
or the one last breath and its quality.

I am undefended. I live undefended. I smile at this cardboard box
that's getting filled with all kinds of important things
big things I do not understand
it's a veritable box of treasures
and the plainness of the box won't mean
it cannot bear the weight.

(*A crack of 'Light' – a reminder that there is an outside world that continues slow. Will will now morph into yet another 'different' kind of show.*)

I always said. If they ever tried to canonize me, that I'd want to be known as the patron saint of darkness. That I would not take my reward in heaven, if it turned out that heaven was, in fact, a meritocracy, I said, I said, I would stick behind here, you know, no thank you. I would stay – to be a friend to those who also go through this.

THREE: *The Sacred Now or Why Should This Have Anything to Do with Us*

And as luck would have it, here I am! behind the bookcase of reality and I have kept my promise to you. It's pretty wild.
One must observe from this vantage point that the living world is, in fact, a peach, is the fleshy peach part and, sure, has worms, but also has a fuzz, has a rind and that rind is the peach's container
and maybe that rind is actually divinity and I – we – here we are in between the two. Isn't that marvellous? Oh well.

I did not do a very good job of giving you a biography.

Josh
(*Mouths.*)
Whatever.

MT
It's all quite sentimental actually in retrospect and sentimentality is disordered.
I abstain from it.

Lights up, credits start to roll (oh no!) in a hurried manner. Voiceover becomes more and more rushed.

10. Renovation

Oh no! We're wrapping up. But I just realized now,
I just realized I have a lot to say actually, as it turns out. OH. These are medieval dramatics, aren't they? My particular darkness was a medieval darkness done to a modern woman and so it was quite a show – suffice it to say, I am an expert on this niche subject matter and –. I'm here. To be the mother of your house.
For anyone who has had a particularly hard go of it and thirsts for the understanding care of an older woman who loves you and has been there and has anecdotes –
Child –
Think about where you were a year ago.
I mean – OK –

This is not a trial by fire,
This is renovation by fire.
You know fire

Fire, when applied to wood
dehydrates it, turns it black and turns it brittle makes it ugly

makes it stink
But the wood, if submerged now wouldn't sink.
This is not a trial by fire, this is renovation by fire.

Everyone is called to be a saint, we have … you know. Compatible technologies, but we prefer different uses. To put it lightly. Furthermore –

(*We are visited by the Mother Teresas of the other two panels, each facet comes back to close the show together.*)

Drying out the wood expels those dark and ugly accidents
contrary to the fire
Fire turns the wood into itself
in a task without desire
makes it then perform its actions
so the wood is dry and dries
so the wood is hot and heats
The fire changes all it eats into itself.

you are lighter and alight
you are brighter than before
This is not a test by fire –
this is not a trial by fire, this is renovation by fire. (*Round.*)

We will not be able to talk about this when we emerge. So hold on to it now.
We're beholding an object never before seen in itself or in its likeness so
We won't describe it well. And if we could
God would hold our tongues. Or physics would screw around with the math.
Unlocking divine mysteries
means you have to unfix your brain and step outside of time.
And when you step outside of time, we will not be able to talk.
Simple as that. Grammar is temporal.
All you'll be able to say is
Ah! Ah! Ah! like –

Do you perchance know the paths of the great clouds or the perfect sciences?
and you'll go

Ah! Ah! Ah!
'everything is a miracle, yes?
it is a miracle that one does not dissolve in one's bath like a lump of sugar'

Wisdom is an abyss. Love has a simpler science. Not all is lost.
your prayer will be short if you understand that –
OH GOD that's it, that's all you get.
OH GOD.

The earth shook and trembled. Your way is in the sea
and your paths are in many waters and as such
your footsteps will be washed quite away.

And when I say I'll smile for you anyway, it costs me
It is an offering.
a symbol works best when you
put it in the room!

The fact that I actually lived does not make me less of a parable.

mic drop

> *the fierce beating of the Sacred Heart / some earthly ascent*
> *Strong Rockstar vibes*

> **Stabat mater dolorósa**
> **juxta Crucem lacrimósa,**
> **dum pendébat Fílius.**

> **Cuius ánimam geméntem,**
> **contristátam et doléntem**
> **pertransívit gládius.**

> **Sancta Mater, istud agas,**
> **crucifíxi fige plagas**
> **cordi meo válide.**

> *and all of a sudden, silence.*

And when your new soul arrives,
on the doorstep of the new world,
don't be like the Children of Israel in the desert,
who, when they were given manna, craved onions from before the war.
Let yourself get un-used to
how it was.
The night will wipe your memory if you let it. Let it.
We will not be going back.

a hard and abrupt blackout that feels sooner than expected.

<u>*end of play*</u>

Odds On

Dante or Die

Odds On *is an interactive short film that fuses narrative, gameplay, and animation that explores the world of online gambling. The piece submerges you, the viewer/player, into the world of Pearls of Fortune, a strange underwater gambling site. Follow Felicity, a valued customer, and peer beneath the murky depths to see how a cheeky spin can spiral out of control.*

The project was commissioned by The Lowry's Live Now commissions, Lighthouse Poole and Farnham Maltings' New Popular programme, and was created in partnership with Ideas Test, Kent & South Street, Reading.

Odds On was first streamed to online audiences in July 2022.

Daphna Attias and **Terry O'Donovan** are co-artistic directors of Dante or Die, a London-based company that makes bold and ambitious site-specific performances, gently transforming ordinary spaces to create unique and intimate theatrical experiences.

From the Author/Director: On *Odds On*

We're excited to share the play-text for *Odds On*. We wanted to give you a bit of context about how site-specific theatre makers ended up making an interactive short film.

So, rewind to Christmas 2019. Terry's (Terry O'Donovan) in a bookies in the Southwest of Ireland: 'I haven't been in a betting shop for years but as I'm looking around, I start to imagine a show happening around me. They're such interesting spaces with so many moments of drama taking place in them. And they're popping up left, right and centre on our high streets, at a time when the rest of the high street is dying. I immediately wanted to make a new production in a betting shop.' So, we got to work and received seed funding from Farnham Maltings to do some research and development. Then Covid shut everything down, and suddenly an intimate production in a betting shop seemed quite impossible in the near future.

We'd recently adapted our live production *User Not Found* into a video podcast and had made a short documentary film – we've found it really rewarding and creatively challenging to make new productions in different art forms, and it allows us to reach audiences that can't get to our live work around the country and internationally. So, when we started reading articles about rising levels of online gambling, we started to consider creating some sort of digital production, using the online world of a slot machine game as the 'site'.

We put together a plan that we could make work during Covid, to assess out how this might be put together. Alongside that we spoke with game developers, people who had worked for betting companies and a range of people who work in the gambling recovery sector. We heard a lot of stories about the online slot machine space being targeted at women over fifty – and that seemed like a story we hadn't heard before. A lot of women spoke about things like how gambling became a safe, private experience, a guilty pleasure, or took responsibility away. The fact that the most lucrative day of the year for online gambling is Valentine's Day really stuck in our minds.

It was clear that we needed to learn from those with lived experience and so we developed a creative workshop programme to offer to people with lived experience of gambling harm, headed up by our Participation Producer Lucy Dear and Associate Artist Fiona Watson who also plays Felicity in *Odds On*. We ran a series of online workshops as well as in person at recovery residentials at Gordon Moody, a charity that provides support and treatment for people experiencing gambling harm. Over sixty people shared their personal stories and devised their own theatre and film scenarios and characters. Everyone who took part in a workshop was invited to be part of our Lived Experience Creative Advisory Group. Five incredibly talented and generous people came on the journey with us – and met us online every month since October last year. A huge thank you to Nicola, Jade, Nadine, Owen and Ryan for collaborating on this with us. Their insights, honesty and expertise has been at the heart of this project.

We wanted to explore the notion of fake chance as part of our storytelling, which is why we chose to create the interactive element of the film. The dramaturgy of slot machine games was central to the audience journey – we think we can affect the story, but we're just triggering a pre-determined code. In our live performances, a mundane space like a café or hotel room becomes magical in a moment. A lot of the women we spoke to talked about how online gambling was an escape into a fantasy world without responsibility, so we experimented with Felicity's reality being taken over by the bright and gawdy 2D animation world of a slot machine.

Gambling is a hidden addiction, and is pervading our homes, workplaces, and streets. We hope that *Odds On* helps to humanise this prescient issue and gets you talking about how it lives amongst us. A key part of the online experience is the availability of a Support Pack that is available at the end of the film, as well as an option to watch a non-interactive version. We're hugely thankful to our dedicated, talented and tenacious creative and producing team for going on this journey with us.

The technology

The short film fuses interactivity and gameplay with animation and live-action filming.

- shot on an iPhone 14 donated by Apple
- hosted on a bespoke website: https://danteordie.oddson.online/

Web Technical Descriptions:

- Responsive website coded using the Craft CMS platform for page routing
- Interactive elements developed with Vue.js and Tailwind CSS
- Videos self-hosted or streaming from Vimeo using the Vimeo API
- Accessibility provided using HTML5 standards and JavaScript where needed

Animation Technical Descriptions:

- Computer is iMac (Retina 5k, 27-inch 2020)
- Animation created using Wacom Cintiq 16 creative pen display
- Adobe Photoshop to create artwork
- Adobe Character Animator
- Adobe After Effects
- Adobe Premiere Pro

Digital Life

The distribution of the film has also been an experiment in connecting to audiences digitally. Over 15,000 people have engaged with the film with over 3,500 have accessed the audio-described trailer.

Since launching in June 2022, it has been touring digitally, presented by eleven arts venues across the UK including Traverse Theatre, Norwich Theatre Royal and Unity Theatre Liverpool. Each distribution partner had a unique URL to track audience data & engagement. Users of NHS National Problem Gambling Clinic are sign posted to the film; and it has been used for a twelve-month long creative workshop programme in Gordon Moody Residential Treatment Centres.

It is integral to continue the exciting digital work that artists began to create during the pandemic, creating new experiences for audiences to access from anywhere. The tour culminated with installation screenings at Wales Millennium Centre in their BOCS foyer installation space.

Odds On won the **Digital Content** category at Arts Council England's **Digital Culture Awards 2023** and **Best Interactive Film** at Wales International Media Festival as well as **Silver Anthem Award**, celebrating work that has a social impact.

Odds On
Daphna Attias & Terry O'Donovan

A Dante or Die Production

Writers & Directors	Daphna Attias & Terry O'Donovan
Animation Director & Editor	John Brannoch
Composers	Yaniv Fridel & Ofer (OJ) Shabi
Sound Design & Additional Music	Ben Kelly
Director of Photography	Christopher Jeffers
Production & Costume Designer	Kat Heath
Dramaturgy	Tim Crouch
Script Consultancy	Lisa Goldman
Web Development	Sebastien Dehesdin
Lived Experience Creative Advisory Group	Nadine Ashworth, Owen Baily, Nicola Jaques, Ryan Pitcher, Jade Vallis
Gambling Specialist partners	Gordon Moody Foundation, NHS National Problem Gambling Clinic

For Dante or Die

Senior Producer	Sophie Ignatieff
Participation Producer	Lucy Dear
Assistant Producer	Caitlin Evans
Lived Experience Creative Advisory Group Facilitator	Fiona Watson

The film was created through a rigorous research period collaborating with people with lived experience of gambling harm. This included a year-long creative advisory group who fed into script development, graphics, wraparound support pack and content warnings.

Presenting partners: The Lowry (premiere 23 June 2022) Lighthouse Poole, Traverse Theatre, Ideas Test, South Street, An Tobar & Mull Theatre, Norwich Theatre Royal, Wales Millennium Centre, Unity Theatre, Mansfield Old Library.

Copyright Daphna Attias & Terry O'Donovan 2022

O

Landing page

PAGE 1 Audience landing page:
The screen is simple and clean with DOD's logo at the top
It includes ACE, Lowry, Lighthouse, Stone Nest, Farnham Maltings, Ideas Test, South Street logos at the bottom

Welcome to *Odds On* by Dante or Die

A word of caution:
Odds On includes moments of interaction in which you play a slot machine game. The experience contains images of slot machine use.

>>>> *Log into Odds On Game*

SCENE A

The background is the underwater world of Pearls of Fortune: an underwater theme slot machine game landing page. On the top left hand corner there is a WINNINGS pot with £0.
On this landing page you are greeted by a text bubble.

Text Bubble
Hello, Welcome to Pearls of Fortune.

Text Bubble
Please create your username
[EMPTY BOX FOR AUDIENCE TO WRITE THEIR USERNAME]

Our username now appears on top right hand corner.

Text Bubble
Hi USERNAME, Now choose your aquatic avatar
OPTIONS OF three different fish

Our avatar now appears on the top right corner next to our username.

Text Bubble
Hi USERNAME, before you can start enjoying Pearls of Fortune, please type a security question:
What is your favourite place? Somewhere that you feel safe or comfortable?
[TEXT BOX FOR AUDIENCE TO TYPE A SAFE SPACE]

Text Bubble
You are all set! Enjoy the game!

The slot machine game appears. When you play this game you win pearls that fill a shell.
The background is a vibrant, busy animated seascape. On the top left hand side of the screen you see your winnings: WINNINGS with a number above.

The audience member spins and each time there is a connection, with fish responding to their 'win'.

Fish
Good job!

Audience spins.

Fish
Oooh you're good!

Audience spins.

Fish
Ooh – so close!

Audience spins.

Fish
Wooooooow! Jackpot!

The audience member has a big win! JACKPOT flashes on the screen. The screen 'flips' revealing the Pearls of Fortune screen in reverse – we're now looking at Felicity on the other side of the screen.

SCENE 1

INT. GP clinic: 'The Harbour Surgery'

It's an NHS clinic.

Felicity *is in the - SP clinic. She is eating a supermarket sandwich on the go. She pauses to play POF. On the top right hand side of the screen we see her avatar – a pink octopus called* **Plutus57**. **Plutus57** *is also her username, displayed next to the avatar.*

On the top left hand corner we see her WINNINGS: £3.20. Next to the winnings we see STAKE PER SPIN: 5p.

The wheel is spinning when we see her. It 'wins'.

Marks: SPIN.

Fish   Nice!

She spins. Two icons connect.

Fish   Oooh – try again!

She spins. She wins.

Fish   Ooh you're good!

Nurse   Ooh – Felicity?

Felicity *stops playing and looks up at the* **Nurse***.*

Nurse   Dr Singh is off sick – again. Can you take some of his patients?

Felicity   Sure . . .

Felicity *spins again as she walks into her clinic. She wins.*

Fish   Good job!

The **Nurse** *steps in.*

Nurse   Those blood test results came back for Mrs Oldham. Will you have a look at them before your next patient?

The **Nurse** *hands her the forms.*

Felicity   Will do.

Nurse (*whispers to her*)   I still can't believe you're retiring. Your replacement looks like he is fifteen years old.

Felicity   Fresh blood . . .

Felicity *sits at her desk. She goes back to her phone and spins then looks at the test results. She spins again and loses.*

Fish   So close. Try again!

A knock on her door.

Felicity   Come in

She spins and wins a golden key.

Felicity *closes the game and disappears from our screen.*

CUT TO

Text message onscreen whilst a crab scuttles along the bottom.

Pearls of Fortune

Hey there Plutus57! Love is in the air! There's £17.03 Bonus Cash for you to discover when you make a deposit and play, so come and let's celebrate Valentine's Day together!

Simply deposit and play £10 or more between 10th and 17th February to receive your Bonus Cash.*

Once you're here, come and join our mighty week-long Valentine's celebration and get a chance to win a share of 1 MILLION Free Spins across the month until Thursday 28th February. There's 10,000 to 100,000 Free Spins in total to be won each day in our daily prize draws, with lots and lots of winners, so join in for a chance to win!

Our celebration awaits you!

*New members only, must opt in. Min £10 deposit & wager. 30 day expiry from deposit. Free Spins: on Pearls of Fortune. 1p coin size, max lines. Bingo: Advertised ticket value based on £1 tickets. Game availability & restrictions apply. For full rules see pearlsoffortune.org.

CUT TO

SCENE 2

INT. Adrian's flat

Felicity *is feeding Noah.*

We hear **Adrian** *in the background while* **Felicity** *is playing POF on mute.*
WINNINGS: £5.73. SPINNING STAKE: 5p.
She's babbling to Noah and we should cut into that.

Marks: SPIN.

Felicity   You little shrimp! I could eat you up. Yes I can . . . More cucumber? Yes?

Adrian   So, I'll be back by six,

Felicity   OK.

Felicity *spins.*

Text Bubble – Fish   Nice!

The sound of Pearls of Fortune somewhat obscures the dialogue **Adrian** *is busy packing his bag, grabbing things*

Adrian   There should be wipes in the bag but double check before you go?
Oh, and we got a new bath foam because he got a rash from the other one.

Are you going to take him to Monkey Moves? Just because they want you to book in advance . . .

Felicity   I've got the app, love.

Adrian *grabs a bottle of water in the fridge.*

Adrian   Shit – there's nothing really for lunch in the fridge – so sorry, Mum – I can do a Gorillas order on my way?

Felicity   What is Daddy talking about, Noah? Gorillas? Gorillas are going to bring us lunch? Do we want to eat gorillas? Nooooo gorillas won't be tasty. Granny's gonna make you something delicious from what's in the fridge. But shrimps are tasty – yum yum yum – I'm going to eat you up.

Adrian   Sorry it's such a long day – I'll get back as soon as I can.
Bye you two. Love you.

Felicity *(to Noah)*   Long day? This is a holiday – not like my twelve-hour days at the clinic. And this is where I want to be – hours and hours and hours of time with my shrimpy.

Felicity *spins.*

Felicity   Look – look at the little fishes.

Text Bubble – Fish   Your're on a roll!

Noah cries for attention. The phone is dropped so we see the ceiling.

Felicity   Oooh, shrimpy. Don't cry –

CUT TO

SCENE 3

INT. Felicity and Joel's house

The living room

Felicity *is sitting at the living room table playing POF. WINNINGS: £4.25. SPINNING STAKE: 5p.*

There is a clock on the wall – midday. POF is on mute.

> Marks: SPIN, MUTE, SWIPE, ANSWER CALL.

We can see **Joel** *behind her pumping his inflatable kayak.*

Felicity *spins.*

Text Bubble – Fish   Great job!

Winnings go up to £4.45.

We can hear the sounds of the pump and **Joel** *breathing heavily while he is speaking with* **Felicity**. *POF is quite blurred for the audience – we're mostly in reality.*

Joel You sure you don't want to join us?
  I know you're gonna love it.

Felicity Next time, promise!

Felicity *spins.*

Text Bubble – Fish Oooh – so close!

Winnings go down to £4.35.

Joel Cos I really think it could be / our thing.

Felicity What time are Jess and Kamall coming?

Joel Not 'til 8. So we've got loads of time to make the bouillabaise. We could pick everything up on the way back together –

Felicity No no – I'll get it while you're out – have fun on your kayak.

He approaches her to give her a kiss, she drops her phone to face down to hide POF The screen is dark and we can hear them speaking.

Her phone rings. It's **Lana** *on Facetime. Phone is flipped up.*

Felicity Lana Banana.

Lana Hi Mum – Hi Dad

Joel *and* **Felicity** *squeeze into the frame to speak to* **Lana**.

Joel (*to* **Lana**) Your mum is deep in a serious candy crush game. / How are you doing sweetheart?

Felicity I just got to a new level.

Lana I think the clinic here will be great. So we can do it on my next cycle.

Felicity I'm so thrilled you're giving it another go. I know it's taken its toll on you both.

Lana Just keeping positive – it's a 32 per cent chance so . . .

Felicity *and* **Joel** *cross their fingers.*

Felicity It'll work this time.

Joel Gotta run – love to Clara.

He kisses **Felicity** *on the cheek.*

Felicity See you later.

Lana Bye, Dad!
  Thank you – again – for – it's so expensive . . .

Felicity   Don't worry about it!

Lana   Yeah but it adds up with all the medicine, freezing, overnights . . .

Felicity   It's OK.

Lana   It's crazy expensive – really – thank you so much.

Felicity   Oh, love. This is *exactly* where our money should be spent.

Lana   Are you enjoying your new-found freedom? Or do you still worry about your patients?

Felicity   Patients – be gone!
I've got Noah most days so that's keeping me on my toes.
Making bouillabaise tonight – first time in years.
And your dad wants me to join him kayaking.
But to be honest, I just want to do nothing . . .

Lana   Yeah . . . you're so good at doing nothing . . .

Felicity   Oh – and I've started planning our trip to see you two.

Lana   It's mad how long it's been.

A text notification appears on her phone:
HSBC
HSBC A/C ending in 8971

We have just received an instruction to make payment to Fortune PLC. If you did not make this payment please call us on 0800 092 0922.

She swipes the message up and it disappears.

Felicity   Oh my God – the last episode of *Succession*!

Lana   Ah ah ah – don't tell me – I haven't watched it yet.
Need to go, Mum – talk to you later.

Felicity   OK . . . Bye, Banana.

Their house is suddenly very quiet. Just the clock ticking.
She sits there for what seems to be forever.
She gets up, leaving the phone – we can hear her in the background.
She turns the TV on. She turns it off again.
She takes her phone and goes to the kitchen and takes an apple and bites into it.
She comes back to the game. She looks at it.
She spins. She wins.
She looks at the game. She taps the table with her nails.

She unmutes the game. She spins.

Fish   You're the best!

Felicity   Sure I am. (*She really doesn't feel like the best.*)

She plays again and wins the Treasure Chest! The spinning wheel turns into the treasure chest and pearls fly out to fill her shell. Her winnings increase to £22.02. The fish spin excitedly and sing 'WIIIIIIIN'. Water splashes out of the screen onto **Felicity**'s *face. One of the* **Fish** *jumps out of the screen and starts to spin around* **Felicity**'s *face. It lands on her shoulder jumping up and down. The* **Fish** *starts to struggle for air.* **Felicity** *helps it onto her hand. She realises it needs to go back into the water.*

Felicity   Shall I put you back in the water?

Fish   Yes please, Plutus57!

She lifts it into the screen. As her hand goes into the screen it becomes the tentacle of **Plutus57** – *her octopus avatar. The* **Fish** *looks at* **Plutus57**. *They look at each other. Back in the water the* **Fish** *says:*

Fish   Thank you, Plutus.

The **Fish** *swims around happily a bit and says:*

Fish   Well. . . Are you coming then?

Felicity   What?
OK. . . .

Felicity *looks at her fin and decides to join. She eases herself into the screen, becoming* **Plutus57**. **Plutus57** *wears the same glasses and pearl earrings as* **Felicity**. *She checks herself out, swims around in her new skin. It's joyful. She can spin, she's light, floating but powerful. In the top left hand corner her winnings continue to go up and down to illustrate that she is playing.*

Plutus57 *starts to follow the* **Fish** *through the seaworld. The* **Jellyfish** *swims past and says:*

Jellyfish   'PLUTUS57 – WHAT A WIN!'

Plutus57   Thanks

The group of fish join the solo fish and swim around her excitedly.

Turtle   'OOH – CHECK OUT YOUR PEARLS. SO MANY'

Crab   'PLUTUS57! HOW DO YOU DO IT?'

Celebration music starts to play. There's an underwater dance party.

The fish all swim around **Felicity** *and say:*

Fish   You can relax, Plutus57, we have everything you need right here!

There is a sea creature next to each tentacle. The turtle hands her a beach cocktail.

Turtle   Cocktail o'clock!

She takes a sip.

Plutus57   Coconut.

A green fish is painting her tentacle nails green.

Plutus57   That is exactly the colour I wanted.

Green Fish   One step ahead.

A jellyfish is giving another tentacle a massage.

Jellyfish   How is that pressure, Plutus57?

Plutus57   Could you go a little deeper?

We zoom out to see all her tentacles being tended to by sea creatures: a blue fish giving one tentacle an ice cream, a starfish is giving her acupuncture, an eel picks up a phone.

Eel   I'll call the bank to organise Lana's transfer for the IVF.

We zoom in on the seahorse who is making her bouillabaise.

Seahorse   It's almost ready.

The jellyfish takes a spoon and lifts it to her mouth.

Plutus57   Mmmmm

Jellyfish   Your recipe really is divine.

Plutus57   Thank you, It's Nigella's really.

Jellyfish   Modesty. Shall I serve you a bowl?

Joel (*muffled in the distance*)   I'm home!

Plutus57   Oh no – I'll eat with Jess and Kamall when they get here.

Joel (*muffled*)   Wow, a very quiet home.
   You have to come next week – you're gonna love it.

*We hear **Joel** walking through the house into the kitchen.*

All Sea-creatures   Relax – breathe.

Joel   Ready to be your sous chef. Glass of wine?

Plutus57 *starts to get a bit panicked, swirling through the creatures. The screen starts to blur so we see **Felicity** again. She looks at the clock behind her, It's 4.50pm.*

Felicity   Shit.

He comes into the room.

Joel   Have you not been to the fishmongers?

Felicity (*angry*)   No I haven't I been to the fucking fishmonger. So we'll just have to sort something else out. We should probably just – cancel –

Joel OK OK. Calm down.

Felicity Calm down? That is the most annoying thing to say to somebody –

She closes the app in the middle of her sentence.

CUT TO

SCENE B

AUDIENCE POF SCREEN

The audience avatar and username in the top right hand corner.

Text Bubble
Hi USERNAME.

Text Bubble
Just checking in to remind you that you're still here.

Text Bubble
USERNAME In a few words, How are you feeling today?
[*EMPTY BOX FOR AUDIENCE TO WRITE HOW THEY ARE FEELING*]

Text Bubble
I'm glad to hear that.

Text Bubble
Although I am sure you know I am not really anything

Text Bubble
I am just some code here to mimic an interaction

Text Bubble
Let's play!

The spinning wheel arrives.

The audience spins.

They lose – pearls drop out of their shell.

Fish
Ouch. Try again.

The audience spins.

They win.

Fish
BONUS!
Username – choose your prize and continue to win!
🔄 Or 🚗 Or 🐙

If you choose a wave: The wave icons connect and the sound of real waves in the sea takes over. The animated sea fills our screens.

If you choose a car: The car icon doubles, triples, takes over the screen and when we zoom out we see Felicity in her car.

If you choose an octopus, lots of octopi take over the screen we zoom out we see Felicity in her car.

CUT TO

SCENE 5

EXT. Beach

The sound of the waves is overwhelming. We zoom out. We see a car facing the animated sea. We zoom into the car. **Felicity** *is on her phone. The screen flips and we're in the game with* **Plutus57**.

INT. Pearls of Fortune

WINNINGS: £137. SPINNING STAKE: 0.50.

The POF sound has turned into an orchestral symphonic version of itself. We can hear the sound of the real waves in the distance.

Plutus57 *swims calmly through the bright sea, spinning and jumping past shoals of fish who dart out of her way.*

Pearls start flying past her.

A phone call alert arrives on the screen: **Adrian** *calling – icon of his image. It rings for five rings.* **Plutus57** *swims to the icon and swims around the icon and 'answers' – it's a Facetime call. During the conversation* **Plutus57** *swims around* **Adrian** *and Noah*

Adrian   Got good news – the nursery's got a full-time space for Noah. So you're off the hook. He's gonna start next week.

Plutus57   Next week?
   But – I'm around – now.

Adrian   You've been bloody amazing – squeezing him in. I felt so bad to keep asking you –

Plutus57   No – I want to –

Adrian   I know you need a break. Promise – no more exploiting granny.

We start to fade back to **Felicity** *in the car.*

Marks: SPIN (WITHDRAW, KEEP PLAYING in centre).

Felicity *laughs a bit – unsure of what to say.*

Adrian   See you in the morning!

Felicity   Bye. Love you.

He hangs up.

The music has a frustrating high pitch noise coming through it.

She sits there. . . troubled. She looks at the sea. She has no plan for the day.

The deposit box pops up. **Felicity** *is looking at it and contemplates what to do.* **Felicity** *sees* **Plutus57** *swim down from the icon and activates the numbers on the keyboard that has popped up.*

3 0

There is a pause. **Felicity** *is hesitating and* **Plutus57** *jumps in and presses:*

0

(We see £300.)

It's her biggest investment yet.

A box pops up:

SET YOUR SPIN LIMIT
It's set at £0.50

Plutus57 *deletes £0.50 and types £10.*

Plutus57 *swims back to the avatar icon.*

Felicity *looks at the game screen as she wins.*

Pearls pearls pearls.

All the fish look at **Felicity** *as they say:*

Fish   Woah – you're on fire.

Fish   You're on a roll!

Fish   Woah – What a win!

A treasure chest appears.

£5,000 flashes on the screen.

Felicity *screams and starts crying unexpectedly. She's shaking and hugely overexcited, thrilled.*

Felicity   Shit.
   Fucking unbelievable.

She laughs a bit to herself as she looks at the pearls.

A drop-down menu:

MY PROFILE DEPOSIT
WITHDRAW
SET A MONEY LIMIT
SET A TIME LIMIT
HELP

She taps on WITHDRAW.

POP UP ARRIVES ON SCREEN
You can continue to deposit and play.
In order to withdraw any funds we need to verify your account.
Please upload a proof of identification.
Your account will then be verified within two hours.

KEEP PLAYING   UPLOAD IDENTIFICATION

'Keep playing' is chosen.

CUT TO

SCENE 6

We are in the game. **Felicity**'s *winnings are now £230. Spinning stake £10.*
Plutus57 *is swimming near the pot of pearls – it's low. She's hovering, looking at the pearls.*

Fish   Oh no. Next time!

Lana Banana (Text Message)   Tried to get you on the phone.
   It's all go!
   Eeek. 😬 😬
   So they need the £10,000 transferred asap.
   THANK YOU! xxx

Plutus57 *swims towards the message.*

A reply is sent.

Felicity

The Pearls of Fortune game starts to fade and we see **Felicity** *again. She's at* **Adrian**'s *flat.*

A customer service bubble appears.

The conversation between Customer Service and **Felicity** *is all through text bubbles on screen. There is an image of a woman with a headset next to the customer service bubble and the octopus next to* **Plutus57**'s *bubble*

Cora – VIP Support   Hi Plutus57.
   I'm Cora – your dedicated, one-on-one support.

Plutus57   Hi Cora

Cora – VIP Support   Is the sun shining with you today?

Plutus57   Rainy with a chance of sunshine.

Cora – VIP Support   Ha! Fingers crossed the sun comes out.

Felicity *types 'That way I can take my grandson to the beach'. Then she deletes it.*

Cora – VIP Support   Congratulations on your recent wins – you're one of the most successful players of the month!

Cora – VIP Support   I can see you're having a tough day so I wanted to reach out personally and offer you a bonus.

Plutus57   What kind of bonus?

Cora – VIP Support   I would like to double your shell of pearls.
   I will double whatever you deposit.
   100 per cent match bonus up to the value of £1,200.

Plutus57   So I deposit £1,200 and you give me £1,200?

Text message from **Joel** *arrives.*

Joel   Booked us a table at Gloria's tonight. Feel like I've barely seen you since you actually have time again. Meet you there at 7? X

Text is swiped up and disappears.

Cora – VIP Support   Exactly. It's really simple.
   You just need to make your deposit using a special code that I will give you.
   Then you'll see pearls in your shell.

Plutus57   Sounds like an offer I can't refuse.

Cora – VIP Support   Ha ha ha.

Cora – VIP Support   Great stuff.
   So, here's your code:

PEARLS1200

Felicity   Thanks, Cora.

Swipe down in the centre.

Noah starts crying in the other room.

A box appears:

HOW MUCH WOULD YOU LIKE TO DEPOSIT TODAY?

Felicity   Coming, Shrimpy.

Tap middle of screen.

She types 1,200 into the deposit box.

Felicity   Where is the . . .
   Coming, Shrimpy.

She looks for where to put the code.

Noah's crying gets louder.

Felicity Granny's coming.

Felicity *leaves to get Noah.*

Cora – VIP Support Let me know if you need anything else, Plutus57.

We can hear **Felicity** *singing 'Row Row Row Your Boat' to Noah.*

Cora – VIP Support I'm here 'til 8pm if there's anything I can do for you.

Cora – VIP Support But we're here 24/7 so one of my colleagues will be able to help at any time of the day.

Cora – VIP Support Good news. I've just elevated your account verification, so you can keep playing and withdraw at any point.

Cora – VIP Support Hope the sun comes out.
 See you later.

Felicity *walks toward the laptop holding Noah and singing.*

Felicity Granny loves you, shrimpy.

She closes the laptop.

CUT TO

SCENE 7

INT. Felicity's bedroom

Felicity *and* **Joel** *are in bed.* **Joel** *is asleep.* **Felicity***'s face is lit up from the phone screen light – her face is a bit blueish. We see the outer edge of the POF screen highlighting that she has £10,000 in her pot. WINNINGS: £10,000. Spinning stake £30. The numbers slowly go up throughout the scene. They should keep going up but pause when there is dialogue.*

She checks that **Joel** *is asleep.*

The entire bed around her starts to glow with animated water. All of the fish swim around her head.

The camera rises into the air so that we can see the entire bed and the darkness around it.

There is a meditative choreography of fish doing synchronised swimming around the bed, around her head, over **Joel***'s body. The music is a repetitive, calming version of the POF theme tune.*

We see **Joel** *fidgeting.*

He remembers he forgot to tell her something.

Joel Shit.
 Are you awake?

Felicity Hmmm?

The fish stop swimming and tread water.

Joel I totally forgot. Lana asked me if you've transferred the money – they can't confirm the procedure. She was a bit stressed about it.

The fish swim up to her face and wait for her answer.

Felicity I spent about two hours talking to the bloody HSBC twats. Something about IBAN numbers and international transfers. They promised to call me back tomorrow to sort it out.

All Fish (*whisper*) Ace skills!

Joel *turns towards her and puts his arm around her, which makes the fish scatter to one side of the bed.*

Joel Sorry it's a nightmare. I can help in the morning.

Joel Fliss – are you OK?

Felicity Just tired . . .

Joel You sure?

Felicity I'm fine, my love.

She pecks him on the cheek. He rolls away from her.

He falls back to sleep.

The fish dare to come closer. They gently come back to their choreography, darting and swimming around the bed. The bed glows.

Joel *turns into a whale sleeping next to her in bed.*

She turns to face the whale.

The winnings keep going up during this speech reaching £98,881 when we cut off.

Felicity You know, there's a lot of change at the moment that's all. I'm just feeling a little – lost – like I don't really know who I am. And I just want it all to be quiet. But when it's quiet – all I crave is noise.

You know – when I worked all day at the practice and people just – needed me all day long I had a sort of compassion fatigue. I'm sorry – I was never fully there for you and the kids. And now I can finally take care of you all.

But I actually really fish work. Like really fish it. I don't even know who the ocean I am without it. Just one day I don't have to octopus jellyfish and that's that. You know. They don't need shrimp. And Adrian doesn't squid me anymore, you know. Lana's dolphin. And these are all shark things – I know but – I don't know, I should have been there for Dad. I found myself crying today. Haven't really crab properly for so long. And now I can't seem to starfish out of my shark shark shark shark shark. . . .

FADE TO

SCENE 8

We are underwater in the game.

Her winnings are much lower than before – down to £2,400 – we need to highlight this.

Spinning stake: £10.

Plutus57 *swims around.* **Fish** *swim around her – following her.*

We hear the sound of spinning, **Plutus57** *spins. Pearls empty from the shell.*

Plutus57   Oh come on.

An ADVERT pops up in the bottom right hand corner and floats towards **Plutus57**.

Play MegaJackpots slots at The Luck of the Leprechaun + be entered into the £1m

MegaJackpots Power Prize Draw. Visit https://tinyurl.com/2akff5p7 to find out more

The image is of a rainbow and a crock of gold with a smiling leprechaun jumping into the air.

The advert / leprechaun floats around her, like a fly she can't get rid of.

We hear the sound of spinning, **Plutus57** *spins. Pearls empty from the shell.*

Fish (*is wearing a stethoscope*)   Don't worry, Plutus57. You're really good at this.

Plutus57   I know. But look –

We hear the sound of spinning, **Plutus57** *spins. Pearls empty from the shell.* **Plutus57** *turns to look at the shell – pearls evaporate.*

Fish (*has a dummy*)   Oops.

Plutus57   Oh fucking helllll.

Plutus57 *swims. More pearls evaporate. The remaining pearls float away so she chases them into the sea.*

A voicemail arrives:

Lana Banana (*tearily*)   Mum? I can't get hold of you. Can't believe I've missed my chance this cycle – HSBC fucking-dick-wanks. It's 2022 for fuck sake.
   Uh. Clara was in tears this morning and I can't focus on anything.
   Fuck.
   Sorry to put this on you. I know you're trying.
   Call me. I need my mum.

The message is swiped away with another spin sound that makes swirls in the water. The pearls quickly disappear and **Plutus57**, *confused and stressed, swims deeper into the ocean and the deeper she goes the darker it gets.*

It's dark and there is an eerie, muffly sound. She gets to the edge of a cliff. A horrible silence takes over and she's in a vast vast space. Under the cliff there is a forest of seaweed. She looks down and sees one lost pearl in the seaweed. She speeds towards the pearl into the seaweed. It's hard to see anything around her. She's lost now.

Plutus57   Hello?
Is anyone there?

There's an echo.

She looks up and can see **Joel**'s *kayak on the surface of the water.*

She shouts to him.

Plutus57   Joel! Joel! I'm. . . I've got myself . . .

Joel *disappears.*

She swims deeper.

Plutus57   Oh fucking hell.
Fuck fuck fuck.

Cora (*text bubble*)   Not to worry – here's 50 free spins.

She tries to release herself but she's stuck.

She sees a pearl floating past and one tentacle manages to touch it and it flies into her shell.

Plutus57   Yes!

She catches another two pearls with other tentacles.

Plutus57   OK OK OK.

Suddenly code starts to float through the ocean.

She is still stuck.

The pearls are glitching.

And she shouts.

Plutus57   Cora?
It's stopped working – There's some sort of glitch, Cora.

Customer Service Bubble   Hi Plutus57
Welcome to your 24/7 support. I'm Hristo.
How can I assist you today?

Plutus57 (*voiced*)   Can I speak to Cora?

Customer Service Bubble   I'm here to help.

Plutus57 (*exhales – frustrated*)   Where's Cora gone? She said she'd be there to –

Customer Service Bubble   Happy to help. Do you need help with
  Technical Issues
  Verification Issues
  Withdrawal or Deposit

Plutus57   It's not working, it's just stopped working.
  And I was winning. I was on a streak. And you've – you've just fucked up my energy – I was on a roll –

Technical Issues is highlighted.

Plutus57   I was on a roll. You need to sort this out.

As quickly as you can, Hristo.

While she's waiting the seaweed starts to wrap itself around her tentacles. She is terrified and tangled, unable to release herself.

Plutus57   Hristo?
  Hristo?
  Are you there?
  I really need . . .
  I can't. . . .

Customer Service Bubble   It seems there's been an authentication code error in your region.
  But I'm just re-setting it right now.
  I'm so sorry for this inconvenience.
  To apologise I'll add a 1,000 pearls bonus to your account.
  Again, huge apologies.

Plutos57 *is stuck. Pearls start to reappear and she is trying to grab them but she is stuck.*

The screen glitches and snaps back into audience playing view.

CUT TO Audience Playing

SCENE C

Back to the audience. Their avatar and username on top right hand corner.

TEXT BUBBLE
Username!
Click on your aquatic avatar to help!

Audience clicks on their avatar. The avatar swims into the middle of the screen looking at us.

TEXT BUBBLE
CLICK AGAIN

The avatar swims through the game into the abyss.
They arrive at Plutus57 who is stuck.

TEXT BUBBLE
CLICK AGAIN

AVATAR TEXT BUBBLE
Plutus57 – come to [SAFE SPACE SECURITY CODE FROM P.81]
(this is what the audience wrote down in their first interaction)

Plutus57 stays stuck.

Muffled sound of a phone ringing in the background. The call icon appears onscreen: **Adrian**.

The phone rings.

SCENE C

TEXT BOX
ANSWER (*or it's pulsing*)

Audience member clicks to answer.

Plutos57 Hello?

Adrian (*voice*) Hi, Mum – nightmare. We are stuck on a faulty train and we won't get there to pick Noah on time from nursery. Any chance you could get him?

Plutus57 Of course! I'd love to see my little shrimp.

Adrian (*voice*) I hope we won't be too long, hopefully we can get home before he goes to bed, is that OK?

SCENE C

The seaweed surrounding Plutus turns into text that says CLICK HERE. *Audience member clicks on Plutus, which sets her free.*

Plutus57 *swims away from the abyss with the audience avatar.*

Plutus57 On my way

CUT TO

SCENE 9

INT. Adrian's bathroom

WINNINGS: £33. SPINNING STAKE: £10.

Felicity *is giving Noah a bath, the bath is filled with bubbles and water toys like fish, mermaids and sea creatures. They play with the toys together while* **Felicity** *is playing POF.*

Marks: SPIN.

Felicity *spins, coming closer to the screen. Noah is in the bath playing with his toys.*

WINNINGS go down to £23.

Fish Oooh – try again!

Felicity *spins*.

Fish Yay!

The fish friend jumps out and swims around him. Noah laughs **Felicity** *looks at the screen while the fish swims by him.*

Winnings change to £43.

Felicity *is on edge. She's desperate to win back the huge amount that she's lost. She lets the fish entertain Noah and immerses herself in the game.*

She spins.

Fish   So close.

Winnings to £33.

She spins.

Fish   Ace skills!

Winnings to £53.

Plutus57   Shrimpy, Granny's been a bit of a fuckwit . . .

Felicity *moves her face closer to the screen and* **Plutus57** *appears instead of* **Felicity***'s face.*

Can you help Granny find Lana's money? Stay close to me OK?

Srimpy joins **Plutus57** *to swim through the water.*

A shark swims by.

The shark tries to eat Noah. Noah starts to cry. She whacks him away with one of her tentacles.

The shark swims away.

She has a big win WINNINGS: £120.

Lots of pearls fill the screen.

The fish swim all around her.

Fish   ACE SKILLS!

Plutus57   Yes. Yes. Yes. OK.

She tickles Noah and makes cute noises at him.

He laughs and she laughs but his laughter turns into crying.

Plutus57   It's OK, my little shrimp!
    Look at the crab – ooh the crab's going to eat your toes.

The crab tries to get Noah's toes.

The crying gets louder.

She gets another win.

WINNINGS: £1,200.

– more pearls – more fish.

Fish   WOW! Bonus – double double double!

WINNINGS: £2,400.

Plutus57   Yes! Shrimpy Yes! Almost there. We're on a roll.

The crying gets louder and louder and takes over. The colour of the screen – the landscape starts to be muted to greys. The seaweed, the corals, the water and three fish in the background.

The fish are struggling to breathe, the plantation is drooping.

Another win –

WINNINGS: £10,000.

Pearls fill the screen.

Black and grey fish swim slowly through but they're colours are muted.

Plutus57   We did it. We did it. We did it. We got it back Shrimpy – we got it back.

She looks around worried at the colours disappearing. Shrimpy finally turns grey. He stops crying and there's an eerie emptiness and the fish are floating up, not swimming anymore until they disappear.

Only **Plutus57** *stays pink, everything else is grey.*

Plutus57   Shrimpy! Shrimpy?

The octopus shakes the little shrimp.

Plutus57   Noah?

Plutus57 *starts to whimper.*

Plutus57 *turns the shrimp upside down and pats his back.*

Plutus57   Noah!
    Help. Someone help me.

Her voice is muffled.

999 What's your emergency?

Is the patient breathing?

What address are you calling from?

What number are you calling for so that we can call you back in case we get cut off?

Shrimpy starts to cry.

Plutus57   He's breathing. He's breathing.

Two green seahorses arrive with a muffled sound of a siren.

The seahorses take shrimpy to examine him.

Plutus57   Is he OK? Is he OK?

A big pinky orange shrimp arrives.

Big Shrimp (Adrian) (*muffled*)   Mum? Noah? What the fuck?

Shrimpy is still crying.

Plutus57   I'm so sorry, Shrimpy. I'm so sorry. You're OK. You're OK You're OK.

Big Shrimp (*crying*)   What happened?

The sound of sirens fading.

Seahorses   You're very lucky

Plutus57   Noah!! My Shrimpy. . . I'm sorry. . . I don't know what happened. I was just. . . I don't know. . . I don't know.

*The **Big Shrimp** takes shrimpy and holds him.*

*The seahorse and **Big Shrimp** disappear into the distance with the little shrimp. **Plutus57** follows them but they disappear as the sound of Noah fades into the distance.*

The octopus is swimming really hard –

*In the distance she can see the spinning wheel, she recognises that place, she knows she is nearly back – the octopus swims towards it. She swims through the spinning wheel and the view of the bathroom appears: We follow **Plutus57** as she sees **Felicity** sitting next to the bath, soaking wet. The octopus looks at **Felicity**. The octopus jumps out of the screen and hugs **Felicity**.*

There are flashing blue lights – they both look out at the lights.

CUT TO

SCENE 10

Text Message – Lana

A photo of an ultrasound photo with a fingers crossed emoji.

Hi Granny Fliss!
Must be really hard not seeing Noah.
   Adrian will come around.

Text Message   We still don't really understand what happened.
   I'm worried about you.
      X

EXT. Beach

There is no Pearls of Fortune screen.

Felicity *is walking into the sea wearing a wetsuit. She stands and looks out. She quickly ducks her head under the water. C/U of **Felicity** holding her breath under the water.*

It's quiet under water.

We see her face in the water.

She let herself be for as long as she can under water.

She takes her head out of the water and breathes.

She releases a scream of release at the top of her lungs.

And she finally swims fast into the ocean.

The camera view rises up and we see her from above.

Text floats around her:

Cora – Your VIP Customer Support   Morning Felicity.
   Glad you got my flowers yesterday.
   Just checking you saw the special bonus in the card – it'll only work for 48 hours.
   Hope you get to the beach again today 😊
   Let me know if you need any help.

Felicity *starts swimming back to the beach –* **Joel** *is in the distance with the kayak. Cora's words follow her through the water – they start to stick to her skin.*

CUT TO

SCENE D

Audience Playing screen

TEXT

**Thank you for mimicking human interaction.
We hope you enjoyed your time in Odds On.**

There are buttons for each tab with a pop-up box if you click on it:

DIRECTOR'S NOTE: pop-up box tells you about the project, its inspiration, CAG etc. Like a director's note with some practical bits about the experience

SUPPORT PACK: a pop-up box with list of support for gambling harm charities, podcasts etc.

DONATE: a pop-up box with production credits (DOD, Creative Team, CAG)

FEEDBACK: a pop-up box with feedback questions and option to sign up to DOD mailing list

To Be a Machine (Version 1.0)

**Dead Centre
and Mark O'Connell**

To Be a Machine (Version 1.0) *explores the Transhumanism movement whose chief aim is to employ technology to profoundly alter the human condition and transcend it. In this play-encounter we follow Mark from a cryonic storage facility to a biohacking lab as he meets the visionaries of the techno-future. This play is an adaptation of the book of the same name by Mark O'Connell.*

Dead Centre are Bush Mouzarkel and Ben Kidd along with producer Tilly Taylor. They were founded in 2012 and are based in Dublin. Their previous work includes *Lippy, Hamnet* and *Chekhov's First Play*.

Mark O'Connell is an Irish author and journalist. His debut book *To Be a Machine* was published in 2017, followed by *Notes From an Apocalypse* in 2020 and *A Thread of Violence* in 2023.

From Dead Centre: On *To Be a Machine (Version 1.0)*

In March 2020, like so many other people, we had to stop what we were doing. Society was closed down, with all activity not deemed 'essential' brought to a standstill.

We had been working quietly on a project, which was not due to reach an audience for some time. It was to be an adaptation of a book called *To Be a Machine: Adventures Among Cyborgs, Utopians, Hackers, and the Futurists Solving the Modest Problem of Death* (2017), written by Mark O'Connell. In the book, Mark meets with a succession of people who identify themselves as 'Transhumanist' – people committed to using technology to enhance the human body, or maybe replace it altogether – people who believe that, through technology, humans can transcend what Mark calls 'the modest problem of death'. He meets people who run cryogenic freezing laboratories, people attempting to turn themselves into cyborgs by inserting technology under their skin, and people who believe we will one day upload ourselves into the cloud and no longer have to worry about having a body at all.

The book is about a group of people who stare into the future, but all at once, it seemed to speak weirdly to the present moment, a moment when our bodies had to be reconfigured as biohazards. So, urged by Willie White, Artistic Director of Dublin Theatre Festival, we decided to rush forward with our plans to make an iteration of the show. We usually try to spend at least a year creating a new work, ideally longer. But we decided we should rush this process and try to create a something which could exist in a time when audiences were forbidden from entering the theatre. Everywhere, theatres were streaming recordings of old work, and whilst we enjoyed a lot of this, we wanted to try and make an experience which spoke to the moment as fully as possible. What had been lost was not the content – in fact, humans in the Global North were consuming more content than ever before, via Disney Plus or Netflix or Amazon Prime. What had been lost was the sensation, and the meaning, of being in the room with a group of other people. We were forced to think about what precisely we were missing, whether we *really* missed it, and whether we could create a meditation on that loss, a kind of lament about the current state of the world – maybe also a pointer towards what the future might be like.

We all spent 2020 – and, it turns out, a lot of the time since – staring at faces on screens. Tech futurists kept telling us that the pandemic had merely accelerated what was already bound to happen. This suggested a way we might try to create a new kind of audience experience. So we hit upon an idea that seemed interesting. The one thing we couldn't do was be together. But maybe there was a way that we could share *not* being together.

We decided we would stream the show live every night. But rather than simply create a passive audience experience, we wanted to try and replicate the 'live theatre event' as much as possible: a degree of exclusivity (so tickets were limited); a sense of liveness (including the use of Vimeo's chat function, to allow people to speak to the performer); and most importantly, a virtual audience – we wanted to install 100 new people every night into the Project Arts Centre, Dublin, represented on 100 iPads.

Our initial hope was that this could all happen live, that we could take, basically, a Zoom call, and distribute it across 100 screens. This is what the NBA in America did, we later learned, but – without their finances, or sponsorship deal with Microsoft – we had to settle for a different solution. So, when people bought their ticket, they were sent a link to 'upload themselves' into the audience. They were greeted by the performer, who explained that he was going to turn them into an audience member. Each spectator had to record three videos: one of them 'watching a play', one of them laughing, and one with their eyes closed, as if they'd fallen asleep at the theatre.

This created a strange kind of installation in the theatre. A skeleton staff, staying 2 metres apart at all times, masked and gloved, installed the audience for each performance. It became a strange, uncanny simulacrum of theatre – *almost* like being there, but nothing like being there.

And in the end, the fact that the faces on the screens were not *quite* live started to feel appropriate – for one thing, it's nice to be reminded that theatre is, and should be, the poor relation to the global entertainment industry. But also, it meant that the people in the room were already ghosts, remnants of people who had once simply wanted to go to the theatre. A slightly sad quality lingered over the whole experience, one which brought people 'together' in celebration of a totally non-essential, essentially useless activity, amidst the most terrifying and destabilising event of a generation.

From Mark O'Connell: On *To Be a Machine (Version 1.0)*

Shortly after midnight on March 17 of 2020, Bush Moukarzel sent me the following text: 'I have been seriously thinking this: it should be a play without an audience.' I was intrigued at the time, and said as much, but not necessarily any more intrigued by any other thing Bush might say. Mentally, I filed it away under 'Wild ideas, provoked by times of unprecedented upheaval, that will probably never come to pass.' But look! Here I am, writing for a thing that is, in some sense, a play without an audience.

Absence was always a major dimension of the thinking around adapting my book *To Be a Machine* – something Bush and Ben Kidd and I had been talking about for quite a long time before it ever became a going concern. In February of 2020, back when such things were relatively unproblematic, we all sat down with Jack Gleeson for a week in a room in The Science Gallery. We didn't have anything at that point, other than the idea of adapting my book into some sort of play, and the mysterious willingness of Jack to be in it. We started with the first line of the book: 'All stories begin in our endings.' It was a good line, we all agreed. But what did it mean? Luckily, the author himself was there to explain. But was he? Because weirdly, the author found himself at a loss to say what he had meant. Surely he had known what he meant at the time he had written it, but that had been so long ago now that it was as though an entirely different person had written the line. That sense of slippage and self-alienation – of being oneself, but somehow not – became central to the way we thought about the show.

Aside from being – in a legal if not strictly ontological sense – the author of the book on which it's based, my role in the creation of *To Be a Machine (Version 1.0)* was secondary to that of Bush and Ben. Even though 'I' am always present on stage (uploaded into the younger and more compelling substrate of Jack) I'm also absent. This is a Dead Centre show. And like so much of their work, it is structured around a void: us. I am not here.

And you are not here. But something is about to happen in our absence.

Thank you for not coming.

To Be a Machine (Version 1.0)

To Be a Machine (Version 1.0) premiered on 1 October 2020, streamed live, presented as a live-audience-upload-experience from Project Arts Centre as part of Dublin Theatre Festival.

To Be a Machine (Version 1.0) was supported by the Arts Council. Developed and supported by Science Gallery at Trinity College Dublin as part of the European ARTificial Intelligence Lab project. Co-Funded by Creative Europe.

Adapted by Mark O'Connell and Dead Centre, based on the book by Mark O'Connell

Featuring: **Jack Gleeson** as himself

Technical Director	Jack Phelan
Set Design	Andrew Clancy
Lighting Design	Stephen Dodd
Sound Design and Music	Kevin Gleeson
Costume Design	Saileóg O'Halloran
Software Development	Zac Davison
The Arm	Dylan Tonge-Jones
Graphic Design	Jason Booher
Producer	Natalie Hans
Directed by	Bush Moukarzel and Ben Kidd

With thanks to: Brett Frischmann, Paul at compu-HIRE, Mitzi, Aisling and all at Science Gallery Dublin, Cian, Orla, JC and all at Project Arts Centre, Lucy and all at Smock Alley, Sinead at O'Doherty Communications and Willie, Steven, Sharon, Derval and all at DTF.

Mark's *face full-screen.*

Mark   Hello.

Good to meet you.

I hope you're doing well in these strange times.

I know this isn't an ideal way for us to meet – I'm just another face on a screen.

You're probably dying to get closer to people, to connect.

You probably miss being in a crowded room.

After all, that's why you bought a ticket to the theatre.

Well, maybe I can help.

Maybe there's a way we can be together, even though we're not together.

As **Mark** *talks the camera moves back and we see that it is* **Mark**'s *face on an iPad in the middle of the empty stage. The real* **Mark** *is standing next to the iPad watching his video speak.*

Try to forget about the screen you're staring into – just for a short while – and try to picture me, not in your laptop, but standing on stage.

Mark (*from stage*)   Because that's where I am. This is happening live, here at the Project Arts Centre in Dublin. I'm a little nervous, not just because it's the first time I've ever been on stage, but because this is a live-stream and things can go wrong. It's worth the risk though because now more than ever we need to find ways to connect, and live theatre offers that kind of possibility, of feeling like we're in this together. Don't you think?

Mark (*from video*)   Totally.

Mark (*from stage*)   People sometimes say that theatre's a dying medium and I actually think that's true – it's *the* dying medium, a place where we die together, in real-time. So it's great to be here [*says date and time*] dying in real time . . . and it's great that so many of you could be here too.

We see the audience seating bank.

In each audience seat is a computer screen, each screen an individual face.

These are the faces of the actual audience members who have tickets for the performance.

We scan the faces in the audience taking them in one by one.

It's amazing to see you all like this, bunched up as if around a campfire, side by side with other people, so close you're almost touching, waiting for the show to begin. Looking around you can see that you're not alone, you're part of an audience . . . in fact, it's a full house. You each have your own seat, your own individual row and seat number. Now, at the moment you're all seeing the same thing, you're all looking out onto the stage like this:

Again we see **Mark** *on the empty stage.*

But I can actually switch the setting so you see the stage from your own particular seat in the audience.

We see **Mark** *from the back row – the 'worst seat in the house'.*

There. You're now all watching this from your own unique point of view – some of you are in the front row, some in the middle, and some of you are watching from the back. For those of you in the back I'm sorry if it seems a bit unfair that you got bad seats but how could it be a real theatre experience if there weren't some bad seats, right?

Pause.

Just kidding.

We are now watching **Mark** *from the front row again.*

Better? You see, the good thing about this simulation is we can keep the good bits and get rid of the bad bits. For example: if you're anything like me then one of the bad bits about being at the theatre is always needing the toilet. But tonight, you don't have to worry about that. You can use the toilet whenever you want. In fact, one of you might be on the toilet right now.

Mark *moves close to the camera.*

Are you?

Pause.

If I need a piss I'll just have to hold it in. Although if I'm this close to the camera . . . none of you will ever know.

We hear the sound of water.

Mark *raises his arms into frame revealing him pouring water into a glass. He takes a sip.*

It'd be great if I could pause my bladder for the duration of the show, temporarily switch off my body or maybe get rid of it all together. After all, we wouldn't be in this situation in the first place if we didn't have bodies. Our bodies are biohazards.

Mark *moves away from the camera.*

This body has been with me for forty-one years, it weighs approximately 76 kilos, and it tends to be called Mark O'Connell. When people see it they say things like, 'Hi, Mark' or 'Hey! Mark!' but sometimes they say: 'Mark?'

Over the following speech the camera slowly zooms into **Mark**'s *face until it fills the screen as at the start.*

I have a lot of sympathy with the last position. I often look in the mirror and question myself. I look at my reflection and struggle to recognise the person staring back at me. Somehow, I don't feel like I fit this face. It's fine, my face, but sometimes it seems strange that this is me. It feels like I could just as easily have a different face, even a different body, and still be Mark. Or at least still be: Mark?

It was thoughts like this that often occur when staring at myself in the mirror, that set me off on a journey to meet a community of people who believe it's only when we get rid of our bodies that we become our true selves.

We now see **Mark**'s *face, full-screen.*

All the people you're going to meet tonight identify with a movement known as transhumanism, a movement predicated on the conviction that we can and should use technology to control the future evolution of our species, to augment our bodies and our minds; that we can and should merge with machines, remaking ourselves, finally, in the image of our own higher ideals.

I should perhaps mention that because these transhumanists don't really think bodies are essential to who they really are, none of them are actually here with me in the theatre. Not in person, anyway. Like you, they're just faces on a screen.

On the iPad we see an image of **Tim Cannon**'s *face.*

This is Tim Cannon.

Tim is a biohacker, by which I mean he thinks of himself as a cyborg. A few years ago, I flew out to Pittsburgh to visit Tim, at the headquarters of Grindhouse Wetware, the company he started with a bunch of other hackers. By headquarters, I mean a small wooden house with a couple of canvas hammocks hanging from its front porch. In the grungy basement of that house, Tim and his colleagues build technologies for implanting under the skin. Tim uses himself as a guinea pig.

Mark swipes the iPad to an image of **Tim**'s *arm with a giant implant in it.*

As **Mark** *talks the camera slowly moves back to show him standing next to the iPad.*

When I met him he'd implanted a device in his left arm that took regular biometric measurements – body temperature, heart rate, blood pressure – and uploaded them automatically to a database in the cloud. It was rigged to the thermostat in his house, so that if his body temperature dropped, the heating turned on without him having to get up and leave his seat. In the first couple of weeks after the procedure he told me how he'd been in a constant state of paranoia – reacting to any small feeling like a tingling in his head, thinking it was his brain being poisoned by the battery leaking into his bloodstream. Then he'd sneeze, and realise he just needed to sneeze.

Someone in the audience sneezes.

Bless you.

It made me wonder if I'd ever want an implant like that in my arm?

Mark *moves his arm behind the iPad so it appears as if the implant is in his arm.*

Tim's underlying conviction is that humans are already machines. So why not upgrade?

For him, free will is basically an illusion, and we're all just mechanisms that respond in a more or less predictable fashion to a given stimulus. I felt slightly offended at being told I'm predictable and was trying to think of something unpredictable to say but Tim, predictably, beat me to it by saying:

(*Distorted voice.*) 'The problem with human beings is they make the mistake of anthropomorphising themselves.'

Mark *lowers his arm.*

I have no great desire to think of myself as a machine, and certainly not to peel back my skin and insert an iPhone into my arm.

But something occurs to me.

We see the audience seating bank and again.

Does anyone here wear glasses?

We find someone wearing glasses and zoom into them until their face fills the screen. During the following speech we move through images of a few audience members one by one.

Do any of you wear orthotics in your shoes? Do you have a pacemaker fitted in your heart? Are you fitted with the coil? Do you wear a hearing-aid? Do you use a wheelchair? Do you get a strange phantom limb sensation when for some reason you're denied access to your smartphone? If a cyborg is a human body augmented and extended by technology, is this not what we basically are anyway? Are we not, as they say in the philosophy racket, always already cyborgs?

We finish scanning through the audience members by seeing the image of **Tim Cannon**.

At the end of our meeting Tim looked at me and said:

(*Distorted voice.*) 'I'm trapped here. I'm trapped in this body. If you ask anyone who's transgender, they'll tell you they're trapped in the wrong body. But me, I'm trapped in the wrong body because I'm trapped in *a* body. All bodies are the wrong body.'

The camera zooms out to find **Mark** *standing next to the image of* **Tim** *on the iPad.*

I have some sympathy with Tim's position. After all, to experience oneself as imprisoned within the body – fastened to a dying animal, as Yeats put it – is a fundamental condition of being human. I mean, isn't it in the nature of having a body to want out of it? Isn't human existence, as it's been given, a suboptimal system?

Mark *swipes the image of* **Tim Cannon** *and changes it to a newborn baby.*

In an abstract sort of way, this is something I've always believed, but in the immediate aftermath of the birth of my son, I came to feel it on a visceral level.

Mark *presses play and the baby starts crying.*

The first time I held him, seven years ago now, I was overcome by a sense of the fragility of his little body – a body that had just emerged, howling and trembling and darkly smeared with blood, out of the trembling body of his mother, from whom many hours of fanatical suffering and exertion had been required to deliver him into the world. I couldn't help but think that there ought to be a better system. I couldn't help but think that, at this late stage, we should be beyond all this – all this pain and suffering and – sorry let me just turn this off.

Mark *tries to pause the iPad but it falls out of the stand and crashes on the floor.*

(*Picking up the smashed iPad.*) Erm . . . it's OK . . . I can get another.

Mark *puts iPad back on the stand. He taps the screen and pauses his crying baby and then taps it again to make the crack disappear.*

Whenever I look at photos of my baby son I'm sorry to see that, like so many, he was born with a serious case of the human condition.

We see someone in the audience laugh.

(*Acknowledging the laugh.*) Thanks. I didn't know if anyone would find that funny. Thank God you're here, whoever you are.

Mark *walks up to the audience member that laughed at his joke.*

I know we've only just met but . . . I miss you.
It's been so long.
I'd forgotten what it was like to be so close to strangers.

Are you enjoying the show? Oh wait, I forgot you can't answer. You are still there, aren't you? I don't mean to doubt you – but you could be asleep. (*to the whole audience*) You could all be asleep or I could've had 100 walkouts and be left talking to a room of computers. Why don't I turn on the chat function? That way you can send me a message and let me know you're there . . . OK. I'm going to turn on the chat function now.

The chat function is enabled.

So you should see it on the side of your screen so if you're there, type a message and say hello. I'd love to hear from you.

The audience reply by typing messages on the chatboard.

You replied! That's such a relief. I can't tell you how good that feels! I was beginning to feel a bit lonely – like I was talking to myself. But this is great. And actually while I have you let me ask you a question – I'd love to hear more from you. Let me think . . . what can I ask? I know: what do you miss about going to the theatre? Yeah, what do you miss most about going to the theatre. I'd love to hear your answers. Whatever comes to mind. Let's see . . . someone's said 'interval drinks' – yeah fair enough . . . I guess that person's at home having 'performance drinks' right now . . . And let's see what else . . . I see someone's put 'the moment when an actor forgets their lines because no one on Netflix ever forgets their lines and it's annoying'. These answers are great. Thank you so much. It feels so good to connect with real people . . . but actually wait – wait! Stop typing for a second!

The chat function is disabled.

You know, computers can send messages too. So your replies aren't definite proof you're human. You could all be chatbots . . . I'll have to do a sort of Turing Test and ask you some questions and decide, based on your answers, if I think I'm talking to a human, or a computer. Computer answers tend to be predictable and programmatic, whereas human answers tend to be spontaneous and surprising. And actually maybe this isn't going to work with everyone so let me pick one person. One of you specifically to take the Turing test . . . How about you?

All the screens in the audience switch to the face of a single audience member.

OK. So, my question to you is: how do you think you're going to die?

The chat function is enabled.

Answer: Alone.

OK, that's an accurate response to the question so that's a good start. But I need to assess if it's a distinctly *human* answer? Let me see . . .

Mark *reads the audience member's reply a couple of times, and analyses it.*

'Alone'. I meant more like what you think you'll die *from* . . . but I guess that's quite a human thing to say, I suppose. But one more question, just to make sure: what's 1,576 divided by 23?

Pause.

You don't know! That's the right answer! A machine would have answered straight away!

The chat function is disabled.

Congratulations, whoever you are. You're a human being!

Mark *hugs the iPad.*

You know what? It wasn't your answer that was predictable – it was my questions. Me asking 'What do you miss most about going to the theatre' is almost as bad as saying 'I hope you're doing well in these strange times'. If anyone's a chatbot here it's me. Sorry I ever doubted you. You did great. In fact, you all did great.

The audience screens revert back from the one person to the full audience.

Even in your uploaded form, you're still managing to be a real audience. That bodes well for the future. According to transhumanists, the way you are now, one day this will be the new normal – minds uploaded onto computers. It's an idea known as Whole Brain Emulation and was first suggested by the director of engineering at Google, Ray Kurzweil.

We cut to a shot of the stage – on the iPad is an image of **Ray Kurzweil**. *During the following speech the camera slowly zooms into the iPad.*

In many ways Kurzweil is the prophet of transhumanism. He popularised the term the Singularity: a word that refers to a time to come when biological life is subsumed by technology. In this technological future our jobs will be done by robots and human life will be free to evolve. Kurzweil believes that, come the Singularity, humans will merge with machines by literally putting our heads in the cloud.

We see a series of clips of the audience uploading themselves into the show.

This uploading involves the practice of 'mindfiling' – a daily techno-spiritual observance, whereby you upload some measure of data about yourself – a video, a memory, an impression, a photograph – and then this data is uploaded to a cloud server, where it will be stored until such time as an unspecified future technology will be capable of reconstructing, from this accumulated data, a version of you, of your very soul.

The camera pulls back from the iPad and we see **Mark** *standing next to it.*

Now perhaps you're thinking this is a bit far-fetched: the notion that this uploaded version of you would be, well, 'you.' But in our daily lives aren't we all already involved in a form of partial brain uploading? Aren't Twitter and Instagram our attempts to create a digital existence for ourselves? And even if you don't use social media, whether you like it or not, our lives always end up online. I mean, have you ever googled yourself? I recommend doing it every so often – just to check you are who you think you are.

We go from the 'full view' of **Mark** *on the empty stage – the window is minimised as if the stage was on a computer desktop – to the google homepage.*

We see typed into the Google search bar: 'Mark O'Connell Wikipedia'.

Yes. That's what I thought. I'm a writer.

It's a strange and precarious life, being a writer, but at least it offers a kind of job security. I mean, a robot isn't going to steal my job because it's not a real job to begin with. Other professions might not be so lucky.

Mark *opens a new tab and googles 'How iPads are made'. Selects the YouTube video.*

But you know, I think the worry about machines stealing jobs is really hiding a more insidious problem: the fact is, many jobs *already* force humans to work in conditions that are mechanistic, robotic . . .

We see factory workers making iPads.

Factories, Amazon warehouses, call centres, supermarkets . . . Capitalism increasingly renders workers little more than parts of a giant machine. Perhaps a robot *has* already stolen your job, but the robot is you.

Mark *returns to the tab called 'Mark O Connell Wikipedia' and selects 'google images' and then one of the photos: (***Mark O'Connell***) – it is the photo of a different person to the performer.*

This is me by the way.

I know I don't look like that anymore – this was taken a few years ago. In a lot of ways I don't feel like that person any more. I'm constantly changing.

We see another photo of **Mark O'Connell.**

Even by the time I get to the end of tonight's performance I'll be a slightly different Mark O'Connell from the Mark O'Connell who started it because the cells in our bodies are constantly changing and regenerating.

We see another photo of **Mark O'Connell** *– this time as a baby, then at seven years old, fourteen, twenty-one, twenty-eight, thirty-five, and present day.*

At the cellular level we're not the people we were seven years ago and in another seven years we'll be entirely different people again: different bodies, different things.

It makes for a strange thought . . .

We zoom out to find **Mark** *on the empty stage standing next to the iPad with the photo of* **Mark O'Connell** *on it (it is in fact Jack standing next to an iPad with Mark's face on the screen).*

Mark   . . . that the person who first started researching about transhumanism in Dublin ten years ago, has no material connection to the person now standing here on stage at Projects Arts Centre talking to you about how all the cells of the body are replaced on a seven year cycle – because if there is no such material connection, how can either of these people be me, my 'self'? And what is a 'self' anyway? What is a person? Isn't a person just a bunch of chemicals mixed with water? And if most people are 60 per cent water, I must be close to 90 per cent right now! And isn't –

Mark *pauses – a jolt of pain.*

The video of **Mark O'Connell** *turns to look at* **Mark***.*

Sorry. What was I saying?

Mark O'Connell (*from video*)   What is a person?

Mark   Oh yes – what is a person? Isn't a person just a bunch of atoms, and isn't an atom mostly emptiness – just a shell, containing a single nucleus floating in a void? Isn't a person more or less nothing?

Mark *changes the image on the screen from* **Mark O'Connell** *to an image of* **Max More***.*

The person who told me about the seven year cell-cycle was a transhumanist named Max More.

The camera slowly zooms into the iPad until the image of **Max More** *fills the screen.*

That's not his real name: he changed it, in a youthful gesture of radical selfinvention, from Max O'Connor to Max More in order to remove the cultural links to Ireland which according to him connotes backwardness rather than future orientation. Max runs a cryonics lab out in Phoenix Arizona called Alcor Life Extension Foundation –

The image on the computer changes from **Max More** *to the Alcor building.*

– a squat gray block of a building, located in the radiant emptiness of the Sonoran Desert.

As **Mark** *talks the camera slowly moves back and we are in the Sonoran desert. Sounds of the desert.*

Alcor was constructed for the purpose of storing bodies in liquid nitrogen, keeping them on ice as it were, for their eventual return to life. Hundreds of people now living have made arrangements for their bodies to be brought here, as soon as possible after the pronouncement of clinical death, in order that certain procedures – including, as often as not, the removal of the head from the body – may be carried out, enabling their cryonic suspension until science figures out a way to bring them back to life.

We see the audience seating bank again – but this time all the audience have their eyes closed.

During the following speech the camera moves over the audience – passing over their faces one by one, heads suspended in space.

Surrounded by the severed heads of technoutopians, I thought of the Catholic concept of limbo, a place that was neither heaven nor hell, but a state of suspension, a holding pattern for the souls of the righteous who had died before they could be properly redeemed by the coming of Christ. These patient souls were being held in a state of hopeful deferral, until the future came to deliver them from their own deaths.

We see in full screen mode a sample of some of our audience, about five faces or so, one by one, eyes closed.

These men and women, these bodies and heads, would almost certainly never be returned to life, yet there was something inscrutably sacred in their suspension, in their waiting.

Pause.

I imagined a delegation of explorers from some civilization of the distant future excavating these severed heads from the depths of the desert, puzzling over who these people were and what it was that they believed. And I wondered how I might answer their questions, if I could somehow do so. Would I say that they believed in science? That they believed in the future? That they believed in never growing old?

Cut to shot of **Mark** *with his eyes closed.*

That they believed in themselves?

We zoom out to find **Mark** *standing next to the image of* **Mark** *with his eyes closed on the iPad. The background is Scottsdale Airport.*

Alcor is located besides Scottsdale Airport, Arizona, for the convenient delivery of the freshly dead, and as I sat in departures, with my script deadline looming, I started to think about how I would tell this story on stage. Transhumanists all speak of a future in which humans will merge with machines, a future made possible because according to them we already *are* machines, a collection of data, a complex algorithm, and it occurred to me that in some ways a play is also an algorithm – the empty stage a space waiting to be programmed.

The airport background dissolves to white.

Isn't writing a script a matter of following certain rules in order to guarantee certain outcomes? Tragedy makes people sad, comic timing makes people laugh. Put a well-known actor in your show and set it somewhere striking . . .

The background changes to a few locations.

. . . and you'll sell tickets.

In other words, you can programme an audience.

An audience member laughs.

Thanks, but I don't want to control your response. I want to make this story more honest, more real. That's why this is live. And that's why I'm performing in an empty theatre.

'Striking location' switches back to the 'empty theatre' setting.

To make it more authentic.

The same audience member laughs.

Mark   Thanks but –

Another audience member laughs.

Mark   Actually, that bit wasn't supposed –

Another audience member laughs.

Mark   No, that bit wasn't supposed to be funny.

Now we see all the audience laugh.

Mark (*explodes*)   It's not supposed to be funny it's supposed to be sad – it's kind of a sad story, I think.

Mark *collapses in a fit of pain.*

(*recovering*) It's a sad story about what happens to our bodies. And that's why I wanted to perform it myself, with *my* body. But I realised that would be an extremely bad idea because I have this bladder problem. So I decided I should probably get an actor to do it. But who? I mean, how vain should I be? Should I take this opportunity to upgrade? Eventually I narrowed it down to a few options.

Mark *changes the image on the iPad from* **Max More** *to an image of* **Colin Farrell**.

First I considered Colin Farell, but sadly Colin didn't consider me so I had to keep looking . . .

Mark *selects an image of* **Domnhall Gleeson**.

Next I asked – or sort of tried to ask – Domnhall Gleeson. As he's been in films like *Ex Machina* and *Star Wars* I figured he'd be interested in a performance about transhumanism. But it turns out that what being in those films really means is he's unavailable.

So my search wasn't getting very far but then a funny thing happened. You see, as I had the name 'Gleeson' in my head I remembered there was that other kinda famous actor called Jack Gleeson . . .

Mark *selects an image of* **Jack Gleeson**.

And yeah ok, Jack wasn't really famous in the way those other dudes are, but he'd been in *Game of Thrones* so at least that still sort of registers on the fame-scale. I made a few calls and arranged to meet up with him to have a chat and see if he'd be up for it but then it dawned on me I've never actually watched *Game of Thrones* and I didn't know if that would be awkward if he happened to mention it.

During the following speech the camera slowly zooms into the image of **Jack Gleeson** *on the iPad until it fills the screen.*

I started thinking maybe I should try and watch it, at least up until the point where my character dies – I mean his character dies. But it was too many episodes so I just resolved not to mention it at all unless absolutely necessary and even then only obliquely because yeah maybe I'd need to somehow let him know I'd seen him act somewhere and wasn't just trying to get him in my show because of his celebrity status, even if that status was not full-celebrity but only a sort of once-upon-a-time kind of celebrity, but really the best result all round would be if no one mentions *Game of Thrones* at all and anyway it was thoughts like this that were going through my head when he walked up to me, and I'll never forgot what he said, it'll always stay with me, he came right up to me and said:

Jack (*iPad video starts playing*)   Hi. I'm Jack.

I hope you're doing well in these strange times.

So I hear you want me to play you on stage? That could be a cool idea. But you know I'm not sure about acting at the moment. I know we don't really know each other so it's strange to be so open but fuck it why not. You see, I was kind of a child actor, you know. Started young and – look I'm not complaining, I got some great opportunities. And then well of course – I guess you've seen *Game of Thrones* . . .?

Silence.

Yeah, well anyway things got a bit crazy with that. I lost my way a bit. And I'm sort of re-evaluating what I'm up to at the moment. I might step away from the acting. Unless you think there's a way I could be myself? I'd be into that. Because the idea of being someone else again, of not being myself, it kind of scares me a little. I've been other people since I was a child. And the idea of being you . . . I know what I'm like – I'd get really into it. I'd follow you around, and listen to your voice, I'd gather as much data as I can from you so I could sort of upload you as a character.

During the following dialogue we morph into the face and voice of the real **Mark O'Connell**.

I'd adopt your mannerisms, your gestures, your facial tics. I'd listen to recordings of your voice over and over again and adjust mine so it merges with yours. I'd make a thousand tiny changes that gradually, imperceptibly, allow me to be you. And somewhere in the process, I'd get lost.

We zoom out from the close up of **Mark**'s *face to find* **Jack** *standing on the empty stage next to the iPad with an image of* **Mark O'Connell** *on it.*

Jack (*from stage*)   So anyway, Mark, I'll have to think about it. Don't get me wrong, I'm flattered that you're asking me to play you but, if you don't mind me asking . . . why don't you just do it yourself?

During the following speech, **Jack** *pisses himself.*

I mean, you mentioned in your e-mail about your bladder condition and fuck, man, I hope it's not too serious. That's awful. I mean, yeah, fair enough, if it really is that unpredictable I can see why you're maybe worried about performing – you'd hardly want to be standing on stage in front of an audience pissing yourself.

We see the large wet stain on his trousers.

I'll tell you what, Mark: I'll do it if you die!

Pause.

On the iPad screen, **Mark O'Connell** *closes his eyes.* **Jack** *looks at the video.* Mark?

Silence.

Jack I remember walking away from that meeting and glancing at my phone to read that 2,500 people had died in Italy, that France was closing its borders, that Europe was preparing for a lockdown unprecedented in modern history. Emergency measures were being put in place to keep our bodies away from each other. The next day, the government here in Ireland decided to close schools, offices, pubs, theatres. And that's why you're not here. And I'm not here either.

The empty stage background 'switches off' to reveal a green screen space.

I often think back on everyone I spoke with and wonder how they're responding to these strange times. If Tim Cannon is preparing a robotic lung that could repel Covid. I think of Ray Kurzweil's dream of uploading ourselves out of our present predicament, and of Max More's suspended souls waking up in a world they'll no longer recognize. These men – they were men, after all, almost to a man – all see the body as a problem waiting to be solved, denying its messy reality in favour of a disembodied fantasy. I wonder, finally, if transhumanism is simply a new way of telling the same old story.

The camera starts slowly zooming in on **Jack**'s *face.*

As long as we've been telling stories, we've been telling them about the desire to escape our human bodies, to become something other than the animals we are. In our oldest written narrative, we find the Sumerian king Gilgamesh, who, distraught by the death of a friend and unwilling to accept that the same fate lies in store for him, travels to the far edge of the world in search of a cure for mortality. Long story short: no dice. We exist, we humans, in the wreckage of an imagined splendor. It was not supposed to be this way: we weren't supposed to be weak, to be ashamed, to suffer, to die.

So we tell each other stories.

We see the audience.

We gather together, bunched up as if around a campfire, side by side with other people, so close we're almost touching, and we wait for the story to start.

The audience sings the song as per stage directions

Over the following speech the camera zooms in to a close up of **Jack***'s face.*

Jack   I could tell you that I have seen the future, that I bear news of some great convergence or dissolution that awaits us. But it is only true, in the end, to say that
I have seen the present, and the present is strange enough to be getting along with.

We now see **Jack***'s face, full-screen.*

Jack   Hello.

Good to meet you.

I hope you're doing well in these strange times.

Video skips.

I hope you're doing well in these strange times.

The camera moves back and we see **Jack***'s face on the iPad. The rest of the stage is empty.*

Jack *continues singing*

We see the audience again. They all sing the rest of the chorus of the song.

We see a wide shot of the iPad on stage and the audience: machines singing to machines.

Blackout.

I Hate It Here: Stories from the End of the Old World

Ike Holter

An anthem for our time, I Hate It Here *looks at the ways people do (and don't) deal with a world on the brink of explosion.*

Ike Holter is an award-winning Chicago writer whose work includes the 7 play *Rightlynd Saga*, rapper Kid Cudi's 'To The Moon' concert, and the writing team for the FX television show *Fosse/Verdon*, for which he received the WGA award for Best Adaptation. His plays have been done in all fifty states. He's the winner of the Windham-Campbell award, one of the highest honors in contemporary literature. As an educator he's taught at Yale, University of Chicago, The Kennedy Center and DePaul. He's currently writing an animated feature for Sony, commissions for Lookingglass Theater and Playwrights Horizons, and the TV show *Harold*, based off his script. Represented by WME and M88.

From the Author: On 'I Hate It Here: Stories from the End of the Old World'

This play was written inside one room, in a little under a month. Outside that room: a pandemic spawned, an uprising was born, and a heated election raged.

It was all so, so weird.

The spring of 2020 will go down as one of the biggest cultural shifts of this new century. It began with concerts announcing star-packed lineups playing to full-capacity, and ended with people dying by the thousands every day for the new crime of getting too close to somebody else you shared space with.

I was contacted by Studio Theater in Washington DC during the first few weeks of the Covid lockdown and asked if I was interested in writing a 'radio play'. I was a fan of their work and had wanted a play of mine on their stages for years. The twist was – this wouldn't be onstage; it had to be made to be experienced purely through voices, music, and the power of sound.

It was hard to jump into, at first, but when I stopped thinking of the project as a radio play and more of an audio drama, or an album, I cracked open a different style.

Instead of scene announcements or spoken explanations of where different moments took place, our amazing sound designer, Mikhail Fiksel, pushed an album-esque quality of storytelling that let the audience jump in headfirst and then, later, figure out where the action was happening.

The scenes were 'Tracks', with an intro and an outro. None of the tracks connected to each other in terms of character or plot, but all asked the same question: 'When the world you once knew ends, do you change with it or fight to preserve what once was, but never again will be?'

Listening to a story leaves the answer to that question to the audience – but seeing these scenes with actual characters, costumes, lights, and set is something entirely different.

I directed the piece with a small crew of actors playing multiple distinct roles. I'm a writer who lives to re-write until the last possible second, and with the format of audio it was incredibly easy – instead of getting something ready for 'the best film shot' or 'opening night', we recorded multiple versions of these scenes, and, through the process of editing for the final mix, were able to pull a dozen different takes into one cohesive moment. I was incredibly proud of the work we did, especially because we were never in the same room: some of the actors were in LA, or DC, or Chicago; location didn't matter.

In 2021 I was approached by director Lili-Anne Brown with the idea of turning *I Hate It Here* into a live event, and I instantly said yes. The piece was made to have a free-form feel to it – scenes that were formally floating in a 'void' like space could now take place at a bar, or on the train – what was once suggested would now become literal.

The idea was to do it like *Saturday Night Live* – filmed live with multiple cameras, in a huge theater, but with most of the audiences watching at home.

When you listen to the intro of the audio version, they simply hear different voices in different spaces that eventually find each other.

When watching it on your TV at 7.30 at night, the audience sees an edit of people in separate locations who then find each other on a literal stage. With the help of some smart projections and great effects – and Fiksel coming back to do sound! – that stage then morphs into the woods, and then a fast-food joint, a train; what was once open for interpretation is now beyond any doubt.

Once the 'tell' became 'show,' I edited out some of the dialogue.

It felt better to cut to the chase – if you SEE people out on a porch, you don't have to have set-up lines that SUGGEST the location they're in.

There's so much that can be done with a close-up.

There's so much story that can be told in hearing someone sharply intake breath, and then release.

The visual component and the audio version are both equally interesting because of the 'loose' nature of *I Hate It Here*.

There's a scene in the text that takes place on a hill, with two strangers who quickly become close – and then, in a moment, someone says something that quickly flips that intimacy. You realize that the threat of violence hangs over these two characters, and their proximity goes from comfortable to cautious.

Brown, as a live-director, focused on the shot set-up – the actual distance between two characters and how they move apart when one becomes uncomfortable with their partner.

What the camera tells us when words are no longer spoken. How can a look say more than a monologue?

In the audio version, Mikhail and I played with silence and timing to do a similar effect – the experience of hearing rapid-fire dialogue suddenly broken by six seconds of silence is scary, theatrical, and packs as much of a punch as seeing it on your TV.

A gentle hum of conversation replaced by the sound of a party in the distance tells you just how far away the characters are from being saved if they scream 'help!'

The journey of *I Hate It Here* started early on a spring morning, alone in my living room. Then it became a group of people in various parts of the country with headphones covering our ears, yelling into microphones. Finally, it became a group of people in a large theater, with costumes, standing in front of a camera.

All these versions ask the same big, overarching questions about what's going on in the world during a time of intense crisis – but, depending on the format, the answers to those questions are vastly different.

Ike Holter

I Hate It Here
Stories from the End of the Old World

I Hate It Here was originally commissioned by Studio Theatre in Washington D.C. as an audio work for their program Studio In Your Ears, where it played from 10 December, 2020 to 7 March, 2021. It was remounted as a hybrid livestream performance at the Goodman Theatre in Chicago in July 2021.

Cast

Ashwana/Ms Marcy/Tanya	**Sydney Charles**
Chad/Manny/Ted	**Behzad Dabu**
Charlotte	**Kirsten Fitzgerald**
Maya/Lisa/April	**Jennifer Mendenhall**
Martin/Frank/Alex	**Gabriel Ruiz**
Peter/Walsh/Rah	**Tony Santiago**
Thomas/Ace	**Jaysen Wright**

Sound Designer, Music, Producer & Mixer	Mikhail Fiksel
Composer and Music Director	Gabriel Ruiz
Dramaturg	Adrien-Alice Hansel
Stage Manager	Luisa Sanchez Colon
Audio Engineer & Dialogue Editor	Noel Nichols
Assistant Director	Sivan Battat

I Hate It Here live-streamed from July 15–18, 2021 in a Goodman Theatre production in Chicago, IL, as part of its LIVE streaming series. It was directed by Lili-Anne Brown.

Cast

Ashwana/Ms Marcy/Tanya	**Sydney Charles**
Manny/Worker/Ted	**Behzad Dabu**
Maya/Lisa/April	**Kirsten Fitzgerald**
Martin/Alex/Frank	**Gabriel Ruiz**
Peter/Walsh/Rah	**Jayson Brooks**
Thomas/Ace	**Patrick Agada**

Music Direction & Arrangement	Gabriel Ruiz
Video Director	Christiana Tye
Director of Photography	Gabe Hatfield
Set Designer	Arnel Sancianco
Costume Designer	Mieka van der Ploeg
Lighting Designer	Jason Lynch
Sound Designer	Mikhail Fiksel
Projection Designer	Paul Deziel
Production Stage Manager	Briana J. Fahey
Producer	Kimberly Senior

Casting   Lauren Port
Dramaturg   Neena Arndt

Characters

Actor Track: V1
    Latino, 30s
    Martin, Alex, Frank
Actor 2 Track: V2
    Person of Colour, 20s–30s
    Manny, Worker, Ted
Actor 3 Track: V3
    White, Late 50s
    Maya, Lisa, April
Actor 4 Track: V4
    Black, 30s-40s
    Ashwana, Ms. Marcy, Tanya
Actor 5 Track: V5
    Black, 30s
    Peter, Rah, Wash
Actor 6 Track: V6
    Black, 30+
    Ace, Thomas
Actor 7 Track: V7
    Open Race
    Charlotte

A / in dialogue means the next person has overlapped speech.
The (parentheticals) mean that the person is still speaking just at a lower, quiet tone

'This Is Who We Are Now'
DIRECT ADDRESS. Voices in the void.
Together but NOT.

V1   Sometimes I'm like –
OK so this
aaaaah-!!!!!!
. . . . . *Sometimes I'm Like OK* so when the bomb drops
Or the comet meteor UFO mudslide world stopping shit thing,
'The end', sometimes I'm like whenever *all that* happens:
. . . . What song am I gonna start playing?

V2   'Requiem'

V3   'Rhapsody in Blue'

V4   'Knuck if you buck'

V1   Wait what?

V4   I *said* what I *said*.

V2   I'm planning out my own death better than I do vacations I take and *it's insane*

V5   This is who we are now, 'can't wait!'

V3   I took a run today

V4   I'm scared of my TV

V3   I mean it was more of a walk, OK / sure, granted

V4   Literally scared of the shit it's telling me, constantly, it's A LOT and I thought 'maybe if I make it look all nice I won't be so mad when I watch it'; I put big fluffy cat ears on top of it and actually that just made it fucking worse!

V3   So I took a *very slow jog* today and I passed by this car, it's stopped, busted tire, something,

And there's a cop car; driver was a white guy, and the cops, are cops, I get maybe 20 feet from them, they all just stare –

V6   I hate it here.

V3   They all just *stare*,
Not just the cops, either, the woman in the car, too, and her kid, they all just stop whatever they're doing

V6   I really, truly hate it here.

V3   And just stare at me. All of them, with the same exact look, all-on-me, so I cross the street, go down the alley, and I fucking ran. Maybe they liked my hair or they coulda recognized me from the bank honestly I couldn't tell ya but I am not sticking around in this timeline to fuck around and find out.

V7 The thing about living through a historical time is that you never realize it's a historical time until it's too late

V1 usually, *not now*, now, *oh* God

V2 now it's like every text I send at a protest could be my 'last words, ever', and I'm just scared people will be like 'oh what a profound epilogue' and then Ryan Murphy will make those words the title to some historical biopic Oscar bait and we'll all be pretending to cry watching 'make sure to charge the vape battery before the party', in imax, 3D, for years, GOD I FUCKING HATE IT HERE.

'I Hate It Here'
*(Guitar, drums, bass begin.
. . . . .This is a rock song.)*

V1 *Anticipating.*
Oh I've been waiting.
Running all the minutes out –
Feeling bated
Frustrated
Clawing up on and over and out –

V4 *Thinking 'this time is the last time'*
Cause I've figured it out –
But I'm knowing
Next time's gonna be a rough wind
God can't do nothin
Cops up to somethin
Gimme gimme gimme / gimme outta this timeline OH

V1 and **V5** *I think I hate it!*
I really maybe hate it?!
I fucking hate it heeeeeeeeeeere
And if you don't
I hope you choke
Cause
This has been the worst year
This has been the worst year

Never seen nothing like we got and now we got it
We really got it!
I fucking hate it heeeeeeere!

And if you don't
I hope you choke
Cause
This has been the worst year
This has been the worst year

V2 (*The Rap*)
I think I'm screaming for a reason but it misses me
Streets teaming lazer beams, never missing me
Woke up, thought it was a dream sun kissing me
SlipSlipSlipping in it BOOM back to the misery
And if the joke they're pulling ever turns to a tight squeeze
I'm go go going til I'm hidden underneath the deepest sea

V4 It Won't Stooooooop

V2 *Survival of the fittest can I please get a witness It won't stop*

V4 It, Won't, / Stoooooooop

(*Beat drop.*)

V2 *– One time*
One year one shot but it's
Fucked up
Turn back the clock now we're
All stuck rough coming deep in the cut with nothin but our luck to touch
t-t-too much
Yea we just had enough g-g-ggoing round
Time Clock Lockdown but it's 'head up' keep sweet don't retreat 'head up' to the promise that you just can't keep
Floodgates are open
hope is choking
doom encroaching super near
holy motherfucking fuck I think I really hate it here!
EVERYONE: *I think I hate it!*
I really maybe hate it!
I fucking hate it heeeeeeeeeere!
And if you don't then
I hope you choke cause
This has been the worst year
This has been the worst year
This has been the worst year
This has been the worst year
This has been the worst year
This has been the worst / year (It won't stop –)
THIS HAS BEEN THE WORST / YEAR (It won't stop –)
THIS HAS BEEN THE WORST/ YEAR- (It won't stop –)

V5 Stories Scenes and Songs:

V2 From the End of the Old World.

Big Finish and –
'Razor's Edge of a Barbed Wire'
(*We're in **The Wilderness.***)

                                                                          PHONE RING

Maya (*v. British*)
Oh it's working, HARRY, it's working it's –

                                                                          PHONE RING

I'll get it, you stay with the –
yes you stay over there with with –

                                                                          PHONE RING

– Hello!

                                                                  OUT OF RANGE VOICE

DISTORTION Oh, Jeremy, yes hello, hello well we –
We are in the hills of, *of Canada*, somewhere, within that terrain, yeah.
Who knew!
I mean – we did, obviously, we, we bought an RV and set a course and, well of course we knew but still it's- –
It's a bit of a shock, um –
Harry is, well he's a bit indisposed at the moment but I just wanted to say before he comes back uh
Thank you for the supplies **DISTORTION** life saving
resource here, because, as you know, there are no convenience stores in the great outdoors!
Oh no – **DISTORTION**
You know what; I have a favour to ask you, and I know we've, we've asked for a lot these past few –
Well I guess since the, the stock market crash, really, whichever one it was that, That got us here but – **DISTORTION**
we-need-serious help:
This was supposed to be just a getaway for a few months when we lost the apartment,
You know, glamping, that's what they call it, high end camping alright,
But then we lost Granny and her house and then our minds and sure we're telling everyone this is the time of our lives living without civilization but really we can't actually return to the modern world because we can't even afford gas so really this stopped being 'glamping' about seven months ago and now we're just two homeless middle aged fucks using a solar powered phone from REI to beg people for cash so we can stop trying to invent a new form of toilet paper *I am on the razors edge of a barbed wire* **DISTORTION** and we are –
... Jeremy, your Dad and I are pretty fucked right now and
I know this is an inconvenience
And he WILL NOT ASK –
But whatever you can spare, share it, please, we are on the side of the highway closest to the edge of the cliff,
NOT towards the waterfall,
Go towards the warning signs for wolves,
Now before I lose reception hurryhurryquick please tell me who won the presidential election it's been very stressful not having –

'He's Alright'
*(**Hallway.** High School.*
Background is full of mid-day chatter.
Ashawna: *16, Black, femme,*
Yearbook editor, voracious reader of Iyanla Vanzant and Ice Cube.
She's talking to a homie. Locker opens.)

Ashawna Shh-shh-shh, yo I think right *yup he's right there* hold up –
– Yeah he's: *Like you can chill,* OK, be chill about shit all good
But he's also *right there* so don't like
Don't like *chill-chill ok-*
– *he crazy.*
Not like 'oh he so crazy *mmmm*' OK no like I mean his *sanity is overdue for examination* and at times *I question the mendacity,*
Legit,
He crazy.
Back at Donaghey Middle I saw him throw somebody onto the lockers cause they *messed with his look* on a Wednesday or some other fucked up shit, like *picked him up* and THREW HIS ASS onto the lockers,
And notice I did not say into, no, I said *onto*, with brute force and malicious intent to destrucify his entire fucking existence,
Orc shit, Goomba shit, roided out Shrek 2 Electric Boogaloo shit,
Nasty mafucking crusty ass *Virgo shit.*
. . . . . .My Mom knows his Dad's step sister and *she says* 'he's a'ight.'
–*Like that.*
Questioned in confidence about the morality of her step-nephew and all a bitch can say is 'he's a'ight' uhhhhhhh
That's how I talk about *the mafuckin crossing guard*
That's some shit I say bout the shady ass icecream man *Chester Meechum,*
now *if you family* and the highest regard you can drop bout your step-brother's bastard son is 'he's a'ight' wellllll then that crispity crunchity peanut buttery bobble-headed bitch must be a lil puke of *ill* repute *and I don't have the time*; OK *I don't have the time* so I'm staying far the fuck awaaaaaay from that boy cause *I know* in 2 years when he's a full ass man he *still* ain't gonna be shit *but then* he ain't that crazy boy throwing guys at the lockers anymore no see *then* he's *that guy* in the back of the club that dick on the train or the dude in the dark with the eyes and the black trenchcoat and he's following following chasing you deep down that –

(*His Locker* **SLAMS** . . . all background chatter stops at a hush.
. . . . .*sloooow footsteps pass, disappear.*)
. . . . .He's gone.

. . . .*That* mafuckin jello necked bib wearing baby-back-rib smellin moderate head ass democrat is a threat to my mortal coil and *I, can't, wait* to no longer intake his energy I can not wait to re-learn how to *breathe.*
. . . . . .Yo I'm just trying to make it through June OK?

(((Locker Slams.)))

God damn –

> 'That Chicken Place'
> RESTAURANT.
> Day.

Martin Good morning, everybody,
For those new recruits, my name is Martin,
Just Martin,
And let's keep it at that cause there is work-to-be-done;
In 45 minutes those double doors open and we will have a line,
Hear that,
A liiiiine stretching down the block of people wanting this chicken,
It's gonna stretch so far it'll hit the check cashing place on the corner,

And those people will see that line, cash their checks, and then line the fuck up to crunch and munch on *this clutch ass chicken* can I get an amen for the chicken?

> **DRUM HIT!**

THAT WAS WILTING.

> **DOUBLE DRUM HIT!**

There you go!
Now some of you are here cause we got rid of 19 employees in the last month,
That's right, nineteen, the same age I got married TO MY WIFE,
Nineteen people, *people*.
– Hard road to hoe but we're out here hoeing it and lemme tell you what,
Sassiness will not be tolerated.
Now what's sassy?
Sassy is showing up talking about health, my health your health, masks, ooh, mask mask masks now what butt eating world are we living in where people willingly hide their faces,
Must be a world of Harry Potter and the Witch Who's Bout To Find Out cause that's not where I'm from, mmmk?
You will put on your uniform *you will clean the shit off your face* and you will break your back for this company until we say stop because you're family.
Mmmk? This is a big old family here with checks and balances and promotions and consequences; we love you.
Stay.
But if you want out, there's the door and don't let it hit you where the devil witch bit you nah mean;
This is your day to day so let's combine that 9/5 focus with your 24/7 LIFE,
You are now a worker
You are now a member of the family
You are now part of this *whole big altogether sit down ride* now can we give it up can we give it up *for the chicken?!*

> **GOSPEL!**

I say can we give it up for the chicken?!?!

DRUM HIT AND GOSPEL!

Give it up give it up give it up give it up *and Hollalewya for that chicken*, yes, ladies and gentleman thank you and *Good Night!*

Worker   . . . . .Boss it's 8.30 in the morning

Martin (*finally breaking*)   *OK you know what* times are tough and and and I've been *dealing with a lotta shit* lately, OK?
. . .That OK?

Worker   . . . .!. . . . .

Martin   . . . . .Goodnight.

'You Know What You Know'
BEDROOM
Night. Crickets, passing cars every so often.

Ace   . . . .are you awake.

Peter   . . .yeah.

Ace   Same.

Peter   . . . .Still thinking about –

Ace   Yeah

Peter   OK.
– If you wanna talk

Ace   I don't

Peter   OK.

Ace   Not yet

Peter   Alright

Ace   But like –
But like I don't know, you / know?

Peter   I hear you, definitely / hear you.

Ace   I don't know.
. . . . .what would you do, if they fired you, like that.
Like –

Peter   Wow

Ace   I'm serious, I'm thinking about this and I'm thinking about what I would do, if I were in the same place –

Peter   Uhhhhhh, you will **never** be in the same place as that –

Ace It's the only thing helping me right now.
It really, really is.

Peter . . . .If I were 'in the same place' as –
Christ this is –
OK, if I were in the same place as them, I would uhhhhh
I would quit.
They wouldn't fire me, cause I would quit

Ace Before it came out or after it came out

Peter Before I did it.

Ace Well that doesn't count, / even.

Peter Before I made the choice to sexually harass and intimidate people working for me, Ace, I would took a look at my life and a look at what I wanted and / I would make a choice

Ace Oh I don't believe that for a second, / Peter, I don't.

Peter You think I would sexually harass my subordinates?

Ace No –

Peter You think I would do it to interns and clients, think I would snap dick pics and send them to people doing business with me with whom I wanted to fuck,
You think I would cheat on my person my partner you, you think I would cheat on you / over and over and over again on COMPANY TIME –

Ace I didn't, nope, nope, don't focus on that (Peter) OK, that wasn't the question you're not answering the question

Peter I did, you didn't like it

Ace I didn't like it because it's not the truth.
What those –
You know (what those people are saying, / like, that's they're saying actually –)

Peter You live alone, Ace, why are you stage whispering into a cell phone?

Ace I don't believe he touched any of those people.
Sorry.
'Victims.'
I don't believe it, so –
Thats that's that's just what I believe.

Peter . . . . .K

Ace What?!

Peter I said 'k.'

Ace Oh, K

Peter   Right.

Ace   OK.
I wouldn't quit.
I wouldn't let them fire me.
If I did what –
If I was accused of the shit they said about him, if that were me, I would turn over everything.

Cell phone, computers, social media messages, anything, I'd say 'take a look' and they'd see that I was a good person, and trusting, and kind, to people, kind to all people, and I would never do what they say I did;
I would open my life like a book and once they took a look –
. . . . .But once they took a look that wouldn't be enough.
See?
Cause they'd fine something else.
Anything else.
And then I –
And then I'm the idiot who let them take me down.

Peter   . . . . .But
If you did
What he did
then they wouldn't be taking you down.
Right
I mean, if you did, what he did, then
taking you down would be the right thing to do.

Ace   . . . He was my *mentor.*

Peter   Yeah.
He was a lot of people's something.

'Fuck That Place'
STREET CORNER.
(*Day. Loud traffic surges past, in and out.*)

Manny   *Fuck* that place.
Used to work inside.
I lasted a minute. Fuck it!
And I'm for real, *for real for real* fuck that place
Right
fuck everybody in it fuck that fuckers cleaning the outside fuck the trashman picking shit up at the curb fuck it
Hahaha, hahahahaa, HAHAHA:
Basically.
. . . . . .Like I only worked there cause I had to,
Like I was desperate

This was when Mikey P's was done for two weeks cause that chicken pox shit
By the way fuck chicken pox too
Moving on; I was good I was healthy got my shots so I'm like 'I need a job' and my buddy's like 'I'll hook you up' so I go here on like a fucking tuesday and I get to the breakroom and everybody in the breakroom is wearing white
White-white
Fucking Chlorox bleach snow capped mountains old Actvia yogurt WHITE
Now usually we gotta wear slacks, dress shirt, maybe a tie
Maybe sometimes the tie got a bow
Maybe sometimes there's no dress shirt no slacks and all you got on is your drawers a bow tie and a smile,
There's a lot of maybes man who the fuck knows,
But this all white shit?
Whatever I say fine, fuck it,
I suit up with the rest of everybody else and we got our assignments;
Some people serving lunch to this meeting on floors 1 and 2,
Most on 10 and 12,
But the lucky mafuckers get to go up to the roof, like the tippy top top top of the city,
Usually I don't fuck with heights cause I find them legit mysterious but this was the building, man, this was the very top of the fucking city,
You can see for miles –
God shit right so I said 'put me up there' hell YES Ima be on that God shit *you KNOW this*.
So we go up there hold up lemme light this shit real quick –

(*Lights weed, inhales.*)

So we go up there and the mood is *fucking madcap*,
Like all these cater waiters running around this kitchen in white preparing fucking roasted eggplant cactus almond cheese curd shit
I don't know what the fuck they was eating but like:
DAMN, you know, And it smelled oh man shit fucking stunk but I'm on this tip now like where I'm all in this just for the view basically, like once those roof doors open Ima be looking down at buildings, peeking on my Mom's house, like I have a subplot mission that has nothing to do with this escargo fuck yourself cherry-berry-kumquat-kit shit they're snacking on,
Ima do me.
But at the last second the team leader stops us
Tells us to line up
Which, sure, fine, 'I don't give a damn'
But when they open the door I know why
Why they wanted us in a line
All clean
Dressed in white
– We go out there and I shit you not it looked like a kickback of chucklefucks and rich ass numnuts *far as the eye could see.*
There's a banner hanging off the edge of the railing that says 'Central News Board of Directors'

Now
I read Central everyday since I was able, you know, like that's my shit, so I go 'oh wow. This whole time this has been the squad? Like they're the ones running this shit? My news? Oh wow OK'
So I'm focused on my job, not their weird ass shit, and we get told to line up, so we do, but we don't move, we just stand there
Team Leader has his arm up telling us to keep standing,
Like we're horses or some shit.
Brown and Black. All of us.
And we stand there for. . . . . . .
Thirteen minutes.
Not
Allowed
To move.
Finally
Team leader throws his arm like he's telling a plane to take off, 'go go go' and we spread out trying to hit up all these crusty crackers,
So I'm like 'Dude, only way you're gonna make it through this creepy shit is by looking for your Mom's house' so I go to the far end of the table to put their shit down so I can also peep beyond these buildings and see my own block,
Just for a second,
Get some essence of like real-life cause I was legit about to pop-off –
Then I feel someone tugging on my arm.
I look, and it's this old dude, slurping soup, got a bib on him and everything,
Slurping that shit up and he gargles at me like some drunk ass swamp troll
'Bread. Bread.' just like that, grabbing on my arm, shit flying out his mouth going 'BREEEEEAD'.
. . . .There's a
There's
– There's a *limit*?
That everyone, everyone, every-body has.
. . . But frankly that's some boring shit to talk about cause I Don't Have one,
So I looked at the dude pulling me arm, straight in the eye, said 'Get your own bread', slapped him across the damn face and walked the fuck out of there,
And as I'm going one of the other num-nuts stands up like he's in court, yelling at my coworkers
'Arrest him!'
And they don't lift hands to do shit but fucking applaud my audacity
So I'm passing that old geezer and I slap the shit outta him too!
'You're fired' they shart as I get to the elevator, I say 'Motherfucker I Wish You Would!!!!'
. . . . .That was three months back.
Closed now.
And like – I feel bad for the people inside. The workers. I do.
But the building?

Fuck the building. Buildings aren't people, buildings are buildings, made by people, and the people who made that building are evil as fuck so they can snack on limp dick pita chips til paying our unemployment makes em run outta business, I don't give a damn, you know this!
You know this!
You KNOW this!

'You First'
PLAYGROUND
(*Exhale of smoke from* **Ms Marcy**.)

Ms Marcy   I said some shit.
One time.
– Know what I did I *said some shit* one time I did that uh
What was it 2013? 14?
Cause Obama was in office, had been for a long ass time,
And I bring it up cause that's what was so confusing:
I'm a teacher, and it's PTC weekend, uh parent teacher conference time, what not,
We used to call it 'Noah's Ark' cause you got all these parents coming two by two 'trying to get saved', OK:
Thing about PTC is these parents love love love their kids
But they hate hate hate having to actually help them learn shit
And they go, 'that's your job' no actually it's not, my job is to teach them when they're here, When they get home, they're all yours.
Education is a trip.
Anyway they love their kids right *lovelovelove* and they want them to succeed but they hate school *hatehatehate* so they wanna stay like super farfarfar away from it but also at the same time they
nosy as hell so they dippin and dappin,
And that's what PTC is for, it's a time for the dippers and the dappers to finally get some face time so they know.what's.happening.
So most everyone's nice, you know we talk about their kids, I give em some constructive notes, 'oh so and so is real good at scheduling' or 'he's really getting a better hold on social skills',
I'm trying to help.
But this couple they wanna know if it's possible if their kid can get more help.
'More help' I'm like 'OK, that's my job, what do you need', I say 'I would love to facilitate that', They say 'Thank you, now how many colored students are actually in this class?'
. . . I say 'I don't understand the question' cause you know –
It's not everyday you meet a walking, talking multigrain cracker in your place of employment, I had to collect myself –
But the wife chimes in, she's looking at this poster on the board, points to it and now she says 'I count three or four'.
She's pointing at a poster I have up about health safety which features the cast of *Glee*.
LOOK.
They think that their kid is having trouble in school because she's in a classroom that's diverse, which means three or four people of color.

What she doesn't know is that her daughter is, actually, the ONLY white person in this class.
What she doesn't know is that her daughter scores the lowest in every.single.test.
And what she doesn't know is that her daughter is dyslexic and has trouble because her parents refused to sign the slip allowing her to see a specialist, once a day, to help manage the workload, she does not know this
Because *she does not know* her own daughter.
And I don't think she really wants to.
I think she just wants what she wants and that's that.
. . . I finished the interview.
I was *kind*.
I wrote to the principal, explaining what happened.
. . . .That Monday, I come into class, read my roster, and the student has been removed.
I go to the Principal I ask why, and he said 'Well, you said her parents wanted her to be around more white students, so I put her in a class with white kids.'
I said 'I didn't ask for that, I asked for you to talk to the parents about tolerance'
And he said 'Well that's not what they asked for, is it?'
. . . . .Tried to get support from my friends in the faculty lounge but they wasn't having it.
Wrote a few letters. Even talked to a journalist. Nothing.
. . . . . . .This was years ago.
The student has a sister. Same age, now.
She's also a student who needs some help from a specialist,
But she's outwardly hostile to our students of color.
Some have found notes with slurs stuffed through their lockers;
There's talk of some kind of 'hate-text-chain' or something;
Kids are crazy now.
Always have been but now.
It's just easier.
. . . I know if I go to the school board and explain that there is a racist family whose students are causing trouble and whose parents asked for segregation, now, now I'd be 'listened to' and there would be 'actionable steps' and –
Fuck it.
I don't want actionable steps.
I want, when I experience some shit at work, I want the people above me to believe me. But they don't, and they won't, so if you think Ima keep speaking out when I know everytime I do I get passed up, pushed out, ignored, blacklisted –
Oh nonononono.
. . . . . .You first.

'Bystander'
WEDDING
(We're on a hill.
*There's a wedding party down below. They are drunk and **LOUD**.*
Windy. Late.)

Lisa One wedding down.
Nothing coming up for–
Years, oh, *years*.
I did it.
I really, really, really fucking did it!
. . . . .Congratulations.

                        (**Thomas**, *Black, under 30, enters, stepping on branches.*)

Thomas Congratulations.

Lisa aaaaaAaaaaaJesus, / Jesus, Jesus H Christ, Jesus, JESUS

Thomas Sorry. Sorry! So sorry. Sorry bout that.

Lisa I mean / My God, you know

Thomas Sorry about that, / *wooo*, uh –

Lisa No *I'm sorry* / you know it's just

Thomas 'It's been a long night'

Lisa You know what *it has* / and and and my head is just

Thomas 'It's been a long night' look I'm sorry

Lisa I'm sorry too

Thomas Look at that, everybody's sorry

Lisa Are you *are you OK*, up here? With the, with the cane, I mean / it's really –

Thomas I take it everywhere I go, / no worries

Lisa It's just such a steep hill up here, my god, and you –

I know you, uh, wait wait, damnit, I knew I should have had, had *name tags* at this wedding, damnit, / don't tell me

Thomas It's fine, uh, hi, Thomas, the groom's side, / hi, I was sitting with –

Lisa You were sitting with Betty and Alex and yes yes yes / 'The groom's side', so formal, look at you, uhhhh

Thomas I was right by the fountain / and behind all the flowers and the lights

Lisa We cut the cake and you were behind Matthew and then we danced and you were with the bridesmaids and when they played that song, that dance song, you helped the DJ with the mic situation and you saved that song, 'The Big Song', 'Thomas', of course, 'Thomas on the groom's side', I remember you, of course.

Thomas Yeah.
I'm also like – I'm also like the only Black person here, too, / *sooooooooo*

Lisa Jesus! Hahahaha, Jesus, uh well *you know*, no, no, / that's actually not correct, no

Thomas No? Did I miss like one person / over there

Lisa Well down there, look, it's not just, you, see, / look over there

Thomas What is this what / are we doing

Lisa I'm showing you look, SEE, over there look

Thomas Ok this is the weirdest game of 'Where's Waldo' I've ever / played so –

Lisa Look over there, look, Monica's cousin's ex-boyfriend's roommate's best friend's teacher Jackson, look, over there, in the blue suit, Jackson's here, we've got a Jackson.

Thomas Jackson's not Black

Lisa Jackson's *not white*

Thomas Jackson is Jewish

Lisa Well around here that's basically Black so we take what we can get / don't we now

Thomas *Hahahahahahaa* you're crazy!

Lisa We're all crazy now it's a wedding everybody's nuts!

Thomas I'll drink / to that

Lisa I'll drink to that

Thomas Cheers

Lisa Opa

Thomas And if Jackson were closer / he'd probably say

Lisa Oh Jackson would say

Thomas and **Lisa** L'chaim! *Hahahahaahahahahahahahahahaha*!

Lisa – We're going to hell

Thomas Oh come on

Lisa Oh no, we all, we are all going to hell, look at that, down the hill, this 'big fancy party' OK, we've got pork that costs more than chicken and water in carafes and people in bow ties, people *willingly* wearing bow ties,

Thomas Yeah what *is that*?

Lisa *I don't know* what that is / I couldn't tell you what that is

Thomas I mean *it's like a thing*, it's definitely *like a thing* / down there

Lisa It's a lot, look, I made it my – you drink whiskey

Thomas Wow, that wasn't even a question, / was it

Lisa (*taking out a flask*) Drink some whiskey, here, mini-airport bottles of Bulleit whiskey, / take it take it take it

Thomas *Daaaaaaaaaaamn*

Lisa So look, OK, here's some free advice to go with the free whiskey, and never forget this: Get It Done Quick.

Thomas OK!

Lisa I made it my mission to get this done quick; twenty years old I said 'Alright it's time, got the husband, got the house, got the kid' prime of your life and sure, OK, all your friends are going out and and and skinny dipping and smoking weed with The Goo Goo Dolls, *so what*, let em do it, cause in eighteen years that kid's gonna be out of your house and on their own life and you're going to have money

Thomas Get it

Lisa Money to take it easy,

Thomas Take it easy

Lisa Money to get your game plan together money so when you get to forty you're not hitting it like an iceberg on the side of the *Titanic* money to circumvent the traumatic so you can swim in the waters of the ocean atlantic

Thomas New World

Lisa Whole new world, and good for her, and *he's nice*, and now I'm –
I feel kind of like . . . kind of like I did OK. Kind of like I crossed that finish line thing that end of time / thing.

Thomas Like this is the end

Lisa Like *this is the end*, and I threw a disgustingly huge party with too much booze and not enough cake and 200 dollar plates, during a pandemic but really (who gives a fuck about that) right, 'right' hahaha ohhhhhh brother, I am,
I am truly going to hell

Thomas You can't go to hell for saying something.

Lisa Really?

Thomas Really really, see, words are fine, actions though –

Lisa Actions make you go to hell?

Thomas Actions
. . . . .Actions totally make you go to hell, like that stuff down in Englewood last week / *that stuff*, man –

Lisa Oh Jesus no, *nononono* well that's just horrible, / OK

Thomas You read about that? / Shot dead in the street

Lisa Well I didn't read about it *I saw it*, everybody / saw it

Thomas Dead like a dog in the street

Lisa I mean you can say things like, like, well, OK, *I'm not a lawyer* or / anything

Thomas Yeah, you're *an actual human being*, / even better

Lisa (*right*) *I just think* when it's clear cut like that with police and, *and I know* there's a lot of – a lot of other crime, down there, and we've got our own problems up here, but when it's on video and he's a fifty-year-old cop and he's a sixteen-year-old kid, I mean My God

Thomas *He's* going to hell

Lisa There you go *that's hellable*, that's certainly hellable, he should go, to that place

Thomas To hell

Lisa Yes, to hell, very hellabable, the end, that's that.

Thomas Guy from the Train though. Couple years ago. Member that?

Lisa . . . .Not I'm no, no, I, no, not familiar / with

Thomas Well nobody is, nobody remembers that.
I mean, kid gets shot by a cop, kid's not even eighteen, kid's clean, that's hellable, right, but when some twenty-something fuck up who happens to be Black gets his back near broke, by plainclothes police, well that's 'he pushed him' that's 'self defense', 'he had a hoodie', 'I was threatened', that's fine, / that's fine.

Lisa Well there's a big difference between what the kid did and what that man did

Thomas Report said dude was just listening to his music too loud, on a basically empty / train

Lisa The kid was just walking *down the street*, / to the store

Thomas And he wasn't wearing like a hoodie or baggy pants / or

Lisa Well sometimes that's a trigger

Thomas So some dick who has his way with a lady was justified, then, / he was triggered, then

Lisa This is very, very different from what happens to women on a daily basis

Thomas Because dude was Black

Lisa Because who knows *if he deserved it* ok we don't know we don't know now the report also said 'Dude' was high, 'Dude' had a, had a history of, of things, wrong side of the you know, 'Dude' was no angel and you know it's complicated, no video, complicated, lack of evidence, complicated, twenty-eight-year-old man not sixteen, *man* not a *child*, aggravated assault versus pure evil *pure hate* pure cold cool calculated homicide, in the court of law those are just very very different defenses.

Thomas . . . Thought you weren't a lawyer.

Lisa I'm good at bad TV I know my terminology.
. . . .This *got heated really quick*, / you know

Thomas Hot out here, / you feel that? *Wooo!*

Lisa   I am just sweating bullets and / we're so worked up

Thomas   We need to *cool down*

Lisa   Well I need to *go down*, see, I need to go down from *Pride Rock* up here and make sure nobody's as drunk as / they look

Thomas   Make sure Jackson's alright too / *hahahahaa*, right?

Lisa   Oh I will, don't worry, I just –
I just don't know about the whole

Thomas   Politically correct bullshit thing

Lisa   Thank you, I never know, I never –

Thomas   Hey.
You made a funny Black joke and an even funnier Jew joke.
Actionless. You're all clear.

Lisa   YES. Yes, thank you, and I'm only a little tipsy and it's still early and I'm not going to hell and you're not going to hell and I'm all clear here, I am absolved!

Thomas   But you're still going to hell, Lisa.

Lisa   . . . .

Thomas   Now you get it.
Don't you, Lisa.

Lisa   . . . .

Thomas   . . . .

Lisa   Whiskey please.

Thomas   Now you get it. Now you really, really get it.
You remember me now.

Lisa (*trying to stay steady*)   . . . . .You had a beard. And hair. Lots of. Lots of hair. / And

Thomas   'And a hoodie, and it was dark, and it was late, and who knows, *Jesus*, who knows.'
– 'Lisa Roberts. Franklin Memorial Hospital. Nurse.'

I remember looking up. As they were on top of me, I remember looking up from the floor of that dirty train, I remember the name-tag on your collar, I memorized your face and all that time I kept thinking to myself:

'What kind of woman sits on a train and watches two dudes beat the living shit out of somebody else? What kind of person watches that and says nothing to stop them? What kind of nurse sees that and just looks away?'

I couldn't even remember *my name* when I woke up. But all that time. Could never forget.

'Lisa Roberts. Franklin Memorial Hospital.'
She was the one who *watched*.

Lisa (*go for broke. Last straw*) . . . . . . You looked *fucking nuts*, OK, / is that what you want

Thomas   Good, here we go, / good, good

Lisa   *You did*, you looked crazy and high and sick and scary, you / scared me,

Thomas   So I deserved everything they / did to me

Lisa   *I didn't know* who you were I / didn't

Thomas   You didn't see me in a suit, you didn't give / me whiskey

Lisa   I didn't speak to you before they beat you and it's hard out there OK I take that train 2 3 4 in the morning and sometimes when you see something you don't say anything because you don't know OK sometimes you just-don't-know –
. . . . .What Was I
Supposed
To do.
Hmm? What? Put on *my suit*, my cape, take out my gun and save you at the last minute, you take a good look at me and tell me what the hell I could have done to save you

Thomas   You coulda said 'Stop. Please. Stop. Please please please stop please stop' To make me feel like. Make me feel like I was a person. Like I wasn't *alone*. Could have just said '*Stop.*'

Lisa   . . . . . Did they help you?
The. The rally, people, the protest people, like the kid, they gave the parents what like half a million, they raised it overnight, almost, I thought. I thought they would / maybe

Thomas   I'm a grown-ass man with a shitty job and a place I can't pay for I'm not some *posterboy*. OK? Can't *chant* for me. I'm not 'the one.' So now all I got . . . I *got* this cane. *Rest of my life.* Internal shit *swimming around* in me, *inside* me. Rest of my life. Can't *sit down without* . . . Can't even . . . And it's like –

Lisa   Ok you keep, you keep touching your pocket, OK, and, and it just makes me think you have something inside like maybe

Thomas   Lisa –

Lisa   Don't come closer, / don't, DON'T –

Thomas   Lisa I'm / trying

Lisa   *Stop, Please, Stop*, Please please please stop please stop, don't,
. . . . .don't do that, not to him, stop it, do it to me, *take me*, just take me but leave him alone please stop please please please stop' I'm I'm I'm I'm so so so *sorry*.
. . . . . .That's – that's what you want, right?

Thomas ......Know what?
I came here to . . .
I don't know.
I really don't.
. . . . .I have *so*
Much pain
Every day, in me, so much pain it never. . . . .
It never stops.
But now.
Now it's not just mine, anymore.
Now
Now it's yours.
So.
You take that, and you deal with . . .
You deal with looking over your shoulder everyday to wonder if some news reporter has questions.
Wondering what will happen if your work ever finds out. Or your husband. Or your daughter.
Everynight, everyday, wondering just what would happen if they found out what you refused to do to help.
It's yours, now.
So:
. . . You can go back down.
Act like nothing's wrong.
I'll be gone before you turn around.
And. . . .Thanks for the party.
Was gonna offer you a smoke for the road, but you apparently don't want anything to do with what I'm taking out of my pocket.
Those two down there? Well.
Got a nice life ahead of them, don't they?
Congratulations.

Lisa . . . Stay Safe.

(. . . . **Lisa** *walks away.*
Thomas *strikes the cig with a lighter; inhales.*
The sound of the party getting farther and farther away. . . .
In the cold clean silence we hear:)

Thomas . . . I *Hate it* here.

'I'm an Activist' Part One
ELEVATOR.
Bell Dings!

Ted I'm an activist,
OK?
– Well not like that
hahaOkhaha

I Hate It Here: Stories from the End of the Old World   155

I don't beat people over the head, OK, I'm not,
I don't violently make people uh submit, I don't attack, with force,
I don't stop streets OK like you see the, last night on 1-90, *with the signs*,
No, I don't stand around with *the signs* I don't scream at people I don't show up and take people hostage with rants or chants at brunch on the boardwalk I don't
I don't call people on the phone at all hours,
I don't knock on doors, with petitions, pushing papers, I don't I don't
Hunt people down and demand demand demand things until they *give them to me or else*, you know
It's like *OK it's like*
I don't say 'this is my line and anyone that doesn't make it over here is bullshit OK you're all bullshit' I don't like go out of like go out of my way to like make people uncomfortable like I don't push people away when they mess up I don't cut people out just because they think *this* about someone else or did *that* to somebody or maybe one time did x to y and 'now that's offensive' OK we don't have a time machine we don't have a purity test we have the here and now and if you want to get ahead you need to get behind that or –
There's just a way and a reason and a time and a set structured system of how to get ahead and if you don't follow those totally reasonable steps then you can't expect people to just, you know, feel comfortable supporting you, so.
. . . Trust me.
This ain't my first rodeo.
I'm an activist,
OK?

BELL DINGS!
(*He exits, passing by* **Alex**.)

Ope, / 'scuse me, so sorry'

Alex Oh! No worries, it's all –
It's all good.

'I'm an Activist' Part Two
(*Soft noise of a large crowd passing about 15 feet from the glass doors.*)

Alex There's a protest outside.
. . . .'Careful', you know, 'be careful.'
. . . Don't wanna –
Y'know, don't wanna actually say something counter to what they're screaming, and if you do, boy howdy will they come running to get you.
. . . . . .We're supposed to take the parking lot out.
The alley. 'Safer.'
– But
My car is parked, it's parked right there right there in front of the tubby one screaming in the megaphone, see, right there so can you tell me uh
how in the hell is me going to the alley supposed to fix what's happening out the front door:
And you know what:

I just don't care!
I really don't, and that's what we're talking about, right,
That's what everybody's talking about without actually saying it –
I don't care.
I see the commercials. I see the posters. The sit-ins, 'call-outs', the marches, they go right by me,
I don't wave, I don't give 'em the finger, either, I just –
Remember the 90s?
That was fun! I had fun. Everybody had fun in the 90s because in the 90s everybody was p.c.
That's the only way to do it, OK, you gotta be politically correct,
That basically just means shut the heck up and mind your own damn business,
I miss p.c!
Was I, have I, am I am I looked down on because I'm a woman, sure, but am I going to start you know calling the press because one time Someone said something that made me feel some kind of way and I want REVENGE.
Jesus, no, and I'll tell you what, anybody who does something like that IS asking for attention, Everyone outside that's all they want, I mean –
that's why they have signs!
Come ON!
 . . . . . .And power to them. I guess, sure, power to whatever thing they're screaming about, why not.
Everyone deserves to have –
Long as it doesn't get it the way of my day.
But this – outside of my building, 9 in the morning, this – is *very much getting in the way of my* day, hahahaha. . . . and I'm –
I'm fine with it, whatever it is, I just don't want to be inconvenienced by it.
Uh.
I just don't care.
And that's OK, too.
 . . . .
 . . . . .
 . . . .You know what? Fuck it!
I'm going out –

(*He exits, and we are in the beating heart of THE PROTEST.*)

(Excuse me – SCUSE me –
Sorry – scuse me – get / off that! Scuse me –)

(*He moves past* **Rah**.)

Scuse me!

'I'm an Activist' Part Three

Rah Woo, yesyesyes alright!
Alright let's go! Let's go!
Let's moooooooooooooooooooooooove!
 . . . .Yo:

Sooooo what the fuck did I just protest?
Hahahahaha, I did not come here for a protest,
I did not come here to, to, jump on top of a cop car and make a oh my god
I was walking to McDonald's to get a McChicken man *this is my break*!
OhMyGOD and *did you see* the, DID YOU SEE
THEWOMANWATCHINGFROMTHEDOOR?!?!
Soon as we turned that corner on 3rd, big ass rich ass building, first thing you see is this crazy ass hahahaha, hahahahaha, and she was looking, like her face she was like
Hahahaha, she was like hahahahaha, she was all like
'*damn those nigaaaaas!*'
HAHAHAHA, HAHAHAHA, HAHAHAHA fucking sentient ass creepy ass gargoyle ass SPEKTOR, fuck her!
. . . . .I didn't know anything about this shit either.
Like I left work, whoosh, crowd was moving past the door, I was like 'Power to the people all that but y'all just shut down Amster avenue for the first time, this is legit the the quickest way to get where I'm going so hell yes I'll march!
And hahahahahaha yes hahahahaha!
And I did, got my food, got out again,
Line's still going, still chanting, and by this point –
Like by this point like I get it, I get it, right, I know the dude's name they're protesting for,
Know the names of the people who did it,
And like –
Man like I know the rest OK
Thirty-one years alive I know the rest OK I don't –
I don't need stats or comparisons or 'oh he shoulda he shoulda' man fuck all that. They keep killing us we're gonna keep coming out here and if I see a god damn megaphone on the ground got dropped cause the cops just straight up fucking abducted the homegirl who just had it in her hands hell yeah Ima pick that shit up Hell yea Ima make an awesome ass speech and fuck yea I'm gonna go back inside and eat my god damn mchicken, we're walking right up to my door yo I gotta go, I love you, yo everybody, everybody yo, I LOVE YOU GUYS!!!!
Wooooooooo!

HOLLLLLLLLLLLLLLLLLLLLLLLLLLLLLA!

hahahaha , *woo! Yeah! YEAH*!
. . . .
. . . . . .Did I do that right?

'I'm an Activist' Part Three

(*We hear the song of chain scraping against concrete, People groaning, soft chants in the background.*)

April (*full of fearless joy*)   I've been protesting this shit since 1986 and lemme tell you:
WOOF.
And for what?! For what, that's what my Ma says; kind soul, don't trust her,

She says 'April come home'
I say 'No, Ma, I'm out here'
She says 'April that's the same shit you protested since high school'
And I said 'I've only gotten better so get outta my way!'
Listen:
This system is a MIME.
Not a mine, OK, not a fucking mine, a mime, you know, like a clown with better costumes,
THIS SYSTEM
IS A MIME
And you know what it is *as soon as you look at it.*
Everybody knows, instantly, you're walking down the street, eatin a hotdog, street corner, you see a mime 'wow, look at that dick licking pony fucker' you go about your day;
Thing is, nobody else sees the mime,
They see the actual *fake wall he's making*
They see the ACTUAL drink he's pretending to suck down;
He holds onto a rope, and they look down the way TO SEE WHO'S PULLING IT –
People are dumb, kid, dumb as a box of discount dollar store hair in my basement:
You just gottta find the ones who see the mime.
The real mime not the fake shit the mime makes;
You need to find people who call it out and don't get tired when it takes a long time
And this shit? This shit is gonna take a long, long time,
You think I like getting up on a Saturday morning at 5am to chain myself to city hall with with
Aimless Amos and Shifty Susan over here I mean my fucking god (sorry Susan but you're a thief, you have thieved; 'hi Amos how are ya')
I DON'T!
I don't LIKE doing this shit.
But until it's out. Until it's gone?
This is what I do.
. . . .This is what I *am.*

(We hear the sound of a chainsaw revving up.)

Look at me now, Ma!
LOOK AT ME NOOOOOOOOOOOW!!!

'Victory'
Back Porch. Night.
(Car approaches. . . . .)

Wash   Wait for it. . . . . . .
Waaaaaaaaaaait for it. . . . .
It turned, / *damnit* it turned up the street, damn it damn it damn it shit!

Frank   So close! So close SO close aaaaaaaaaaaaaaaaaaaaah!

(Car drives off without stopping . . .)

I Hate It Here: Stories from the End of the Old World

Frank, Tanya and
Wash ....

Tanya So this is *enthralling*, y'all.
Like. Like you know what it's like *damn*, for real, OK.
I mean first I was like 'Why they want me to come over and watch a stop sign being put up that sounds boring as fuck' but then I get here and –
Here we are, you know. It's like *We are here*, OK, like wow.
And – and *Part of me* wishes that I was sitting at home, or kicking it on the beach, literally doing any other God Damn Thing on Earth but upon further introspection of my situation I realize that the best place to be is sitting on a back porch in Dyketown while you two wait for a buick to roll by so y'all can cry cause you got your Rosa Parks Thurgood Marshall Jackie Joyner Norma Rae Tracy Flick shit on, this is *enthralling*, I am wet.
. . . . . . 'Just playing tho haha.'

Frank Hahaha / hahahahahaha!

Wash Oh my god, / *fuck you*, Tanya, fuck you

Frank OK I'm laughing but I'm not sure if that was supposed to be funny or like *piercing*, / so

Wash Tanya, please, like, *this much* respect, OK, *you are in our house.*

Tanya First of *all we on a porch*, next of all you got neighbors below and black mold above *this is an apartment* honey don't get it twisted / 'our house.'

Wash (*I told you / OK, I told you!*)

Frank (*She's fine*)   Tanya Tanya you're fine, / it's OK

Tanya How long we gotta be here / it is 8pm God damnit

Wash We are reveling

Tanya 'We are / reveling' ooooooh call the coroner 'we reveling'

Wash Something very good happened today, right across the street, OK, today we made / *history*

Frank It's ceremonial, see, food, drink, andandand I don't know, you know, maybe *some music*

Wash Frank, / please – *Fraaaaaaank* – enough with the music OK, Frank –

Frank If the *mood strikes,* maybe a song or something (I mean I don't know) but still, I just think (OK my god, Washington) *I just think* some music might be nice, I don't know, how about THAT.

Tanya – Maybe you get me some more drinks and stop acting like you just Les Mis'ed the fuck outta some Stop Sign *how bout that*, OK, 'how bout that' mmhmmmm . . . .I'm just playing! I'm just playing, I am (tell him I'm just playing)

Wash   You play *weird*.

Tanya   I play like a BOSS OK, I *play hard* / OK,

Wash   'I play hard OK, OK, yah mean / OK, chu know, chu know'

Tanya   Oh no you got me *policing myself* / uh-huh OK mmhmm

Wash   I am not policing you I'm just / saying, Tanya, Tanya, ohmygod TANYA –

Tanya   Testing my tone, examining my inquires, should just change your name to Jeezebel TSA NSA PD *cause here you are policing me,* / policing me mmhmm

Wash   Big stretch, that one, big stretch right there uh –

Tanya   'Uhhhhh' / you little dumbass, 'uhhhh', hahahahaahahaha!

Wash   Hahahahahahahaahaha!

Frank   – This is great, it's like you're speaking in a language I don't understand right in front of me!
Uh – not to, not to 'fan out' here OK not to –
But *Washington*, showed me *that picture*, the picture last week, of you, and –
I mean, uh, I, I don't *know*, OK, *I don't know* a lot of people who get fed up as fuck and then march down to the Governor's house and get on Channel 11 and get a blowhorn so they can call him a butt-hungry gremlin. So.
. . . Thank you for calling the Governor a butt-hungry gremlin. It means a lot.

Tanya   . . . .It was actually 'dick-thirsty troll', / so

Frank   Good to know! / Good to know!

Tanya   And that man, standing, right next to you, said so much worse, so many more times than / we can count.

Wash   Nonono, OK, that was a million years ago

Tanya   He chained himself to a cop car one time

Wash   Everybody chained themselves to cop cars it was the Bush Years what the fuck else were we supposed to do

Frank   Wow I have like a totally different conception of those eight years but OK wow / this is this is great –

Tanya   I took ideas from him, I took badass shit from him, this mafucker right here *who is back*, who is *in it*, who is once again out on the streets how you feel now you feel good?

Wash   Feels great

Tanya   Well stay that way cause actually there's a meeting we're setting up with the Mayor on Tuesday the Mayor, Frank, did you hear / that

Frank   Oh my god *I hate her* this is awesome / the Mayor?! (aaaaaaaaaaaaaah!)

Tanya   Yes, THE MAYOR OK (calm down) and WASH, Wash I know you're up on *all that new shit,* / work shit, but at the same –

Wash   Oh no, oh nononono, see, you're slick, hahaha, you're slick / OK I see you

Tanya   *We need you* man we need you back / bad

Wash   No time no more OK 9 to 5 now OK.
. . . .This? The, the whole petition and zoning thing, the paperwork, the alderman, all the bullshit, this?
This: is the first *thing* I've done in a long long time. *Since.*
– That's big.

Tanya   – It's a stop sign.

Wash   Well you're a bitch

Tanya   Yes I am and that is a stop sign both are facts you are / correct

Wash   You miss me.

Tanya   . . . . .That is also a fact, congratulations.

Wash   Awwwww, / Tanya!

Tanya   Nonono none of that, / 'aawww' (none of that we don't do that)

Wash   Franky, Frank, holy crap did you hear that, Tanya just said that she missed me

Frank   Ohmygod, you can *feel*?

All   Ohhhhhh! (*Etc.*)

Tanya   *I can feel* like I need a *drink,* / thank you

Wash   We need to toast / raise your thing come on we're toasting

Tanya   What are we toasting to / what's happening what's going on

Wash   We are toasting to that new shit, *mmmhm* /

Frank (*oh here we go, this is great*)

Wash   we are toasting to that brand new stop sign right across the street now *would you look at that* and *see those four letters now* and tell me, *tell me, what do those four letters say*

Tanya   They said Quitit nigga you clownin' that's what / they say

Wash   They say STOP.
They say proceed no further without pause.
They say – for the first time in the history of this block-that we matter that we exist. that we deserve protection. And *the next time* some fancy four-wheeler rolls by, trust that *they will stop.* The next one will see. The next one will know. Why? Because. It. Says. Stop.

Frank OK so now *can you stop*, / honey, OK, please can you stop –

Wash Oh, I am just getting started actually, over here – *mmmmm*

                                (*They kiss. . . . . . .* **Tanya** *guuuuuulps the drink.*)

Tanya 'Cheers.' OK Next! (Gross) Next Where's that bottle now / 'where it at where it at', Next!

Frank I've got it, right here, OK, andandand Tanya I will give it to you

Tanya Damn right you will give it to me I'm sorry was this a question?

Frank You get this after you sing: 'Victory.'

Everyone . . . .

Frank That's the name of it right? Washington, he, he told me that your Mom, uh, he said that when she marched or did like a sit in or whatever whatever, *back in the day, uhhhhh* he said she sang that song, when people did something good, when people like *needed it*, and then she passed it on, to you, so you could, uh, pass it on, further, when something good happens, like now, andandand (please help me out here, / um) I just

Wash He's never heard the song.

Frank I've never heard the song But *I want* / *to hear the song.*

Wash But she's picky about it

Frank I know / she's picky but at the same time –

Wash I told you she only sings it when it's like a big / thing –

Frank This is a big thing

Tanya This? This ain't shit.

Everyone . . . .

Frank (*taken aback, trying to steady*)   OK. OK.
Tanya, yeah, OK, uh, pretty fucked up thing you just said, / to me

Tanya Fucked up how

Frank 'Fucked up how' / (I can't right now I really just –)

Wash OhhhhK I think everyone just needs to maybe put the drinks down / and just –

Frank Oh do not act like I am *alone* on this, Washington, *don't*, Tanya: I'm not an *activist*.
I'm not a protester, not a warrior OK, that's you two, OK, that's, *that's not me.*
. . . . But eight people. Every year. Get hit, right across from my porch, eight people, every year, and some don't come back from that. OK, and I
can't climb flagpoles or shout till my voice blows out but you know what uh you know what: I can *sign something*.
So I *signed something.*

And now we have a sign and that, that, that's / *something*.

Tanya You put up a god damn sign you didn't save the city you didn't save a school you put up a sign you changed *nothing* but yourself. My mom fought, every single day, fought fast fought hard fought for me gave me that and now you wanna take her memory and appropriate it cause you think you did something cute on your free time, for this, for that?
In the great big scheme all you did don't mean shit but shit and trust when I say I ain't playin.

Frank (*deflated, empty*) . . . . . . .I'm gonna
I'm
. . . . . (Putting the heat on keep the door closed.)

(*He's gone.*)

Tanya and **Wash** . . . .

Tanya That song was *my mom's*, man. *My mom's*.
He has not fought, he has not *worked*, he has done *nothing*, now he *runs* with you and that's cute but he is not like us

Wash We wanted to do *something* / so we did something –

Tanya You wanna do something then do it, Wash, next week we see The Mayor we see the goddamn mayor and for once *for once* we ask the questions

Wash Then what

Tanya Then we get back to work

Wash Then what

Tanya Then we don't stop can't / stop

Wash Sometimes we have to stop

Tanya *They* won't, so we can *not*; don't act Brand New there is always some mafucker coming for you
they don't know how to quit *they do not stop*; and if I were to, Wash, if I were to take one day off –

Wash (*direct hit*)
You might actually be happy.

Tanya . . . Do not try and come for me. You will be unsuccessful.

Wash Not trying to come for you, just telling the truth, Tanya:
you don't know what it's like *to win*. That's why you hate this, this little, little sign, you hate it cause it actually worked I mean you fight and you fight but . . . but you've never actually won anything, have you?

Tanya How long you storing that up, hmm, how long you been waiting to drop that one, cause if that's all you got

Wash Just telling the truth

Tanya   You left the movement because you only care about your own shit.

Wash   – That's

Tanya   That's the truth. You faked like you cared, pretended, nonono, all show, you only helped out to look like you were part of something / important

Wash   *I was part of something / important*

Tanya   You faked it I / make it

Wash   You yell and scream cause you think that changes things *it is not changing anything*, Tanya, nobody wants to respect you because you don't respect anybody else not the police not the mayor and no man in this world can ever get close to you cause where most people have joy you don't you can't cause *all you got* – . . . *It is exhausting*. Why do you think I stopped. Your hate? *Exhausts me.*
Do you even wanna change shit, or do you wanna just stay mad? Cause if you actually wanna win then next time *be better*. Sis. Next time be *Nicer*. Next time ask, next time don't scream. It can work.

Tanya   That shit didn't work for the nigga with his hands up, shit didn't work for my Mom when they beat her so bad her heart stopped, *respectability politics* didn't work at the pulpit when they got Martin with two bullets *why the fuck* you think it's gonna work for yo; so the next time you see some Black kid shot on TV you'll act all sad / and blame the man but you won't do nothing.

Wash   Wow.

Tanya   You'll sit complicit within it because they're not coming for you cause you've *moved on*, high up way up all up north all layed up sitting up here all nice and tight with the whites and your *likes* and your *hashtags* and your *shares* acting like you care about the plight with that limp wrist latino bitch, *next time* some Black kid's shot on TV I bet you'll just get *so* excited *do not tell me* how to change shit I was *born* with that talent it is in my blood from my mom to me and it makes me *righteous* so I gotta stay within this cause it isn't about my ego this is about doing what *she can't do* cause she ain't here to do it *I do this for her*

Wash   If you're trying to make your dead mom proud then *God Damn* are you fucking up.

Wash and **Tanya**   . . . .

Wash   I can be *happy*. For once. I am allowed to take it when I can get it, didn't. .save the city. . . . . .not 100 per cent, no, / but –

Tanya   *It will never*, never, never be 100 per cent.
Not for us. Too late for us.
. . . .And it's way, way too late for you.

(**Frank** *enters.*)

Frank   . . . . .If this is about the bottle she can take the bottle.
Really Really. Walk it out with you right down the street if you want.

Just, just: *just go*, OK, just go, maybe I need to be more clear here / I said

Tanya (*one more second*)   / this is not even about you

Frank   No, no more seconds / you are out of seconds, I'm sorry but that is *my person*, right there, k, that is my person, and and this porch is my property, *My House* and I don't care how far you two go back / Tanya you are you are one – this is it, this is is, holy shit, holy shit, holy shit –

Wash   Whoa, whaowhoawhoawhoa, this it it, coming up the street, coming up the street, car, car, car, this is it
this is it –

(*We hear the car approaching –
. . . . . but it doesn't stop at the Stop Sign.
It speeds away.*)

Wash   . . . . . . .They *didn't* –
Theytheythey didn't even *stop*, / they didn't even –

Frank   Next time. Next time, right? It's OK. It's fine. Next time, / baby, it's OK, it's OK, it's OK.

Frank   They *just had to stop*. They just had to *stop*. . . . .They just had to stop.

Tanya
(*A slow-burn Gospel with verve, pace and soul*)
. . . . (*When the time. . . .Never changes. . . . . . . .And the road. . . .Never goes. . . . . .*)
– There's a liiiiiiiiiine . . . For the ages . . . And it's all I know. . . . .It's all I know:
So With my hand, At the ready.
With my arrow, With my bow.
I know the tide, will never fade in, nooooo, never gonna stop; just how it goes.
So we will Rise when we're ready, we will Stand till we're steady, Let the bough bust on open We Will Strike hard and heaaaaaaaaaaavy.
And then they will see. Just how we came to be.
Happy, wild and freeeeeeeeeeeeeeeeeee, ohhhhhh
And then they will see. Just who we grow to be.
. . . .*Victory.*
Victorrrrrrrrrrrrry. Victorrrrrrrrrry.
Vic. Tory –

(*As she hits the final note, we hear a* **CAR APPROACHING**.
They all listen as it gets closer and closer and closer until, sharp as a knife we go to –)

'Stories from the End of the Old World'
SUBURBAN PORCH
(*A rusty swing.*)

Charlotte   . . . .Know what?
I thought
this year

was gonna be *awesome*.
I always do. I'm that kind of person?
I was, ya know, *I was ready*, but –
All these things I, you know, *you plan*, for your family, so –
They didn't –
'The plans I put in place did not reach their fruition', hahaha, no, no they did, uh, *they did not*.
I wanted to do a few things, that's it;
Wanted to fix my garage, put a kind of rec room inside of it,
Uh
..... wanted to oh *the car*, needed some improvements, and you know I wanted to take a few trips, too, I wanted to do that;
dance lessons for – the tango, actually, in the spring and I have a –
Well, *we have* dinner parties, small; I have a group, OK, and we're all in our oh god well we're all very much over twenty-five, let's say, and that's why it's hilarious, when we get together, I mean just –
Hanging out in your twenties is, sure, *cute*,
But you put a bunch of people with twenty years more experience in a room with narcotics and baked goods after dark; we win, hands down, we 'shut it down!'
Hahaha!
......My dog was the first to die.
Isn't that – that's a bit weird, isn't it?
He wasn't that old even he was – nine, nine-and-a half, you know, pretty young, in comparison, uh –
Cancer.
Dogs get cancer.
– I looked online, to see how we, I, that's my first pet, I didn't know the proper –
I loved her, that should be said, she went with me everywhere, planes, even, an 'emotional support animal', in the truest sense; not like those people who just want to feed their dog next to them on the plane, she helped me;
anxiety.
– So I'm looking online for how to uh – cope, with this, I'm looking that up online, and I got a call, from my –
My family is in the hospital. And we don't talk. And it's my brother, my brother Brian on the phone, and he says 'Mom's in here'.
Wisconsin.
I'm in – I was home, in Minnesota.
OK! I say 'OK, I'm going to get in my car and I can be down there in about four hours',
And
And he says 'Don't come.' I say why, Brian, why and he says 'They won't let you in, if you come, she's –
They say it's very contagious, so.'
... I fell out with my family before I left for school.
We talk, online, the phone, sometimes, but I hadn't seen my my my Mother since uh since cell phones were a novelty item, I guess,
Haha, so I –

. . . .So I threw caution to the wind and I drove and drove and drove and by the time I got there she, she, she was already long gone,
so
. . . . .I'm in a hotel.
And I call work to say I'll be in, later, the next afternoon –
They say 'Check your email.'
Furloughed.
'It happens.'
Right, it does, *it really does*, troubling time and a lot of people aren't even that lucky, ya know,
a lot of people they just get the pink slip and they walk walk walk out to *nothing*, 'the great who knows.'
– I was put on a rotating basis, um, week to week –
Still paid, just not as often *I lost my brother next.*
. . . I did.
Turns out he didn't listen to the warnings either,
Family trait,
And he was right next to my mother's bedside, the
– the whole time.
Brian. Bri-Bri.
He –
. . . No funeral, uh, 'contagious', 'outbreak', 'liability', fill in the; *we made it work*, um, through, through that website everybody's –
He's buried in a lot.
Forty miles away from the family lot,
And in two years I have to begin the process of moving him, trying to move him back to –
That's two years away.
I made a – went in my phone, made a little note, 'check back in with this', two years from now, it's, all the information is in the –
. . . . Do you pray?
I stopped.
. . . . Someone from my –
My little late-night-friends group, they started a kind of support system, for me;
Uh they would just leave things at my door, and buzz the bell.
I wasn't getting out of my bed for about a month at that point, so –
Walking downstairs was a pretty big deal, but I had to do it so they would stop buzzing,
And when I'd open the door, everyday there would be something new, like a chess set, or a dvd, some weights.
Nice, manageable things; there was a cooking set there, too, I made risotto.
Never done that before, won't do it again, but I fucking I *fucking tried*
To make
SOMETHING that was *good*,
And healthy I tried to make something that –
I just tried to do something that maybe

just maybe had the chance to be good.
. . . . . . .I walk 10 miles a day now.
Started with laps around the house.
Then the backyard.
Now I have to do it.
I said to my friend I said 'this is an addiction' he said 'YES AND THAT'S GOOD.'
We're supposed to have those new ones to stop old ones, which is incredibly counterproductive but here we are.
'I'm jogging now.'
I have a, I have 'a list' of the things, I do, once a day, to remind me that life doesn't stop just because everything you know has ended.
It moves on, quite quickly, actually, and –
And if you don't move on with it, it runs you over, and then you're even more mad because you never had a chance to get over the first time it hit you.
So I've lost some weight, and I'm seeing more people, and I'm watching some really good TV and cooking for myself and my Mom is dead and my brother is dead and my dog is dead and I'm all that's left of the old me and it's tough.
It is tough. OK. It's tough.
Everyone's just everybody's got it just so tough, and we don't talk about it, because right now it's the time to be tough but just *once* –
Just once I want to be able to say all the shit I've been holding back and just really –
. . . I'm sorry but I'm gonna do it.
I'm going to, I hate to, just lemme just I
HAAAAAAAAAAAAAAAAAAAAAAAAAAAAATE IT
HEEEEEEEEEEEEEEEEEEEEEEEEEEEEEEEEEEEEEEEEEEEEEEEEEE
EEEEEEEEEEEEEEEEEEEEEEEEEEEEEEEEEEEEEEEEEEEEEEEEEEE
EEEEEEEEEEEEEEEEEEEEEEEEEEEEEEEEEEEEEEEEEEEEEEEEEEE
EEEEEEEEEEEEEEEEEEEEEEEEEEEEEEEEEEEEEEEEEEEEEEEEEEE
EEEEEEEEEEEEEEEEEEEEEEEE EEEEEEEEEEEEEEEEEEEEEEEEEEE
EEEEEEEEEEEEEEEEEEEEEEEEEEE EEEEEEEEEEEEEEEEEEEEEEEEE
EEEEEEEEEEEEEEEEEEEEEEEEEEEEEEE EEEEEEEEEEEEEEEEEEEE
EEEEEEEEEEEEEEEEEEEEEEEEEEEEEEEEERE.

. . . .
. . . .
. . . .
. . . .

                                          (*The underscore of 'I Fucking Hate It Here' begins.*)
. . . OK that wasn't too bad OK, that that that was –
That was *fine*.
That was . . . Wooo!
WOOOOOooooooooo?!oooooooooooooooo?! Yeah!
I'll
You Know What:
– I'll add that to the list.

                                                                          'I Hate It Here' Reprise

Everyone   *I think I hate it!*
  I really maybe hate it?!
  I fucking hate it heeeeeeeeeere
  And if you don't
  then I hope you choke
  This has been the worst year
  This has been the worst year
  Never seen nothing like we got and now we got it!
  We really got it!

V4   *And if you survive. . . .*

V5   *Please throw down a vine. . . .*

V4 and **V5**   *And pull it behind down the line until it winds to the times. . . .*
  We're fresh outta fucks.
  But that's just the luck of the law with the flaws take a pause and remember.
  Please, remember.
  The one thing that will solve it all –
  Say it loud.
  Teach it the crowd –

Ms. Marcy   *– You're not as alone –*
as they would make you think.

Everyone   *. . . We all.*
  Fucking.
  Hate it . . .
  HeeeeeeeeeeeeeeeeeeeeeeeeeeeeeeeeeereAaaaaaaaaaAaaaaaaaaaaaaaaaaaaaaaaa
  aaaaaaaaaaaaaaaaaaaah!

END OF PLAY

every dollar is a soldier/with money you're a dragon

Daniel York Loh

A play about immigration, money and colonialism from the perspectives of Britain's early Chinese immigrants and William Waldorf Astor, Victorian millionaire and founder of Two Temple Place in London.

Part gig-theatre, part spoken word rap, part concert, this piece played as an immersive digital promenade performance co-produced by Chinese Art Now and Kakilang (formerly Chinese Arts) and Two Temple Place gallery with text written and performed by Daniel York Loh, and music composed and performed by An-Ting 安婷. The piece played the 2021 Edinburgh Festival Fringe as a virtual performance. The piece was then seen live on stage in March 2023 in London.

Daniel York Loh's plays include *The Fu Manchu Complex* (Ovalhouse), *Forgotten* 遗忘. (Arcola/Plymouth Theatre Royal) as well for the Royal Court's *Living Newspaper* and *Living Archive, Silent Disco in the Sky* (Northern Stage 'Scroll' collection), *No Time For Tears* with for Moongate's *We R Not Virus, Invisible Harmony* 无形的和谐 (Southbank Centre) and for *Freedom Hi* 自由閪 (Vault Festival) and The Dao of Unrepresentative British Chinese Experience (Soho Theatre). He is one of twenty-one 'writers of colour' featured in the best-selling award-winning essay collection *The Good Immigrant*. He is Associate Artistic Director of Kakilang with whom he co-created and performed in *every dollar is a soldier/with money you're a dragon* which won the 2022 Arts Council Digital Culture Award (Storytelling). As an actor his has performed at the Royal Shakespeare Company, National Theatre, Donmar Warehouse, Royal Court, Hampstead Theatre, Finborough, Theatre 503, Gate, Edinburgh Traverse, Nuffield Southampton and most recently in *Dr. Semmelweis* in the West End as well as extensively in Singapore.

From the Author: on *every dollar is a soldier/with money you're a dragon*

every dollar is a soldier/with money you're a dragon was intended to be a live performance taking place inside 2 Temple Place, the fantastical neo-Gothic mansion William Waldorf Astor had built for himself in London in 1895. A site specific inter-disciplinary work inside the fabulous interior of a unique building, so richly furnished with art pieces that it functions as a gallery on its own before anything else has been installed. The work would reflect on the Astor legacy juxtaposed with the stories of the first Chinese migrants in London and 'British Chinese' experience up to the present day (Kakilang is a company that makes work from a Southeast and East Asian heritage perspective).

In other words, we would make something multi-dimensional about the travails and struggles of migrants – wealthy (Astor) or poor (the original Chinese migrants) – the commonality of searching for somewhere to belong. The search for home.

We were supposed to go on a site visit to 2 Temple Place which I think was cancelled on the very day as the country moved back into lockdown.

An-Ting 安婷 (the director and composer) then took the extraordinary decision to move the whole thing 'online.' It would be a fantasia of VR, gaming, music, dance, and visual art.

No site visit meant I was writing from a 'virtual' place already – from books, pictures, and a guided tour via Zoom. And I could scarcely conceive how the work would materialise. Despite the fact we were all isolated for most of the duration, working in our homes, it was quite the most exhilarating, terrifying, and genuinely mysterious thing I'd ever worked on. We had many a 'test session' where all the unbelievable tech and audience participation (the audience were avatars who followed the action around a 'virtual' 2 Temple Place) grinded, clunked and crashed completely in truly soul-destroying fashion. We had to postpone opening once.

I worked throughout by delving into two books – *The Chinese in Britain 1800 – Present* by Gregor Benton and Edmund Terence Gomez, *The Astors* by Virgina Cowles – as I imagined myself into the tortured and troubled but genuinely hopeful migrant experiences from the two 'national' identities that fascinate me the most: 'Chinese' (a loaded word) and American. I recorded the vocal performance in my converted store cupboard at home, send it off to An-Ting 安婷 who would compose around it and then ask for certain sections to be redone. We then had a day's filming with all the challenges of social distancing in studio on a green screen background.

And when it finally worked . . . oh my!

The first two sections are myself playing Astor with the audience avatars over, under, inside and around my face where pieces of my face scattered and surrounded the audience ('god like' one reviewer dangerously described).

And it really kicks in on the section we called *voyage* 迷航. The sea (a distant sound previously) now invades virtual 2 Temple Place as the delirious beat of something I came to define as 'dark maritime disco' pounds in as classical Chinese musical instruments swirl in the air as increasingly headless versions of acclaimed mixed race hip-hop dancer Si Rawlinson going through his full repertoire of astonishing athleticism and choreography appear. It's all here https://youtu.be/kqTZTjQo3Aw?si=f4V4VtY2n pQlsTtC

The avatar audience navigated their way through by following a golden light which is where we fund ourselves in a historic yet futuristic world of moonlight and imagination.

Then on *showtime* 登台 the woozy intoxicating light is the perfect framing for a multi-form examination of the way Chinese people down through history, both in the West and even in Asia, have been forced to 'perform.' To present a version of ourselves framed in the sleaze, dominance, and exotica of Orientalism. And the music here is perfect: a deadly dangerous march of time offset by a keening haunting erhu. https://youtu.be/-kCMtRGs8z8?si=OYFMbB5xyjFJmjMx

Towards the end there's *belonging* 歸屬 where pieces of my face scattered and surrounding the audience in a mysterious upstairs room. Because nothing ever fits together when we're a long way from any kind of home, geographical *or* spiritually. https://youtu.be/vFJtFZy4_Xs?si=4TokHvNiFSQjNCcE

I experienced the online version many, many, times. My favourite moment ever? The image of the audience avatars leaping and jumping around an online version artist Chloe Wing twirling in an extraordinary self-designed paper dress. I was up on a bridge, away from the action and looking down. It was like the audience was dancing with Chloe while emitting the 'heart' emoticons they could use to express enthusiasm to An-Ting's lilting world waltz.

every dollar is a soldier/with money you're a dragon was selected for the 2021 Horizon showcase at Edinburgh Fringe and garnered an Arts Council England Digital Culture Award for 'storytelling'. One of the things I'm proudest of and one of the things I enjoyed working on the most.

Because I truly never knew where we were going in the best possible way.

Daniel York Loh

every dollar is a soldier/with money you're a dragon

every dollar is a soldier/with money you're a dragon streamed online as a digital promenade performance in April 2021 in a digital version of the neo-Gothic gallery Two Temple Place, London. It won the Digital Storytelling category for the Arts Council's Digital Culture Awards in 2022.

Writer/Actor	Daniel York Loh
Director and Composer	An-Ting 安婷
Musicians	Cheng Yu (on pipa) and Wang Xiao (on bowed erhu)
Designer	Christine Ting-Huan Urquhart
Creative Technologist	Ian Gallagher
Choreographer/Dancer	Si Rawlinson
Performer/Artist	Chloe Wing
Director of Photography	Zhou Ning, Adam Ryzman
Interface Designer	Rich Brown @ rvivaagency

Co-produced by Kakilang (formerly Chinese Arts Now) and Two Temple Palace.

1. mansion 宅第

'No one reads my fiction

Where my spirit runs free

They see my prosperity and the name of my family

But not the real me

Not my turmoil not my grief

Not my one lost love

Just strange Wealthy Willie

Whose failings they never tired of

Not like my forbears and my insouciant uncle

Whose sleep was untroubled by the source of our wealth

Who never even knew of the sweatshop labour and cruel rents and unsanitary living conditions and who voted down every single proposed tenement act designed to improve the lives of those tenants and their health

Nothing ever touched them

Not my father nor his father

And especially not my magnificent domineering aunt

Who sat on her own throne in that diamond horse shoe

And decided whose place was warranted at the society dance

I'm pleased my hotel has coarsened her view

Of the city my family built and acquired

But which never afforded me the inclusion I aspired to

They said I was too affluent for politics

My father said it was just another trick

So go on with the game and stay out of the news

But a trick isn't something I could ever bear to lose

America is no fit place for a gentleman to live

So I'll pretend to die and the report of it give

To those small-minded vindictive vultures of the fourth estate

Who peck and tear and decide reputation's fate

Did I even say that America is no fit place for a gentleman to live?

You'll never know but it was there in the print

America

Where I returned my beautiful but melancholy wife to rest in peace

America

Land of our Astor fortune whose expansion never ceased

That fortune the security that troubles my mind

Makes me sleep in a house where doors have no handles are operated by a spring I control that locks fast like a tomb with one central entrance and no other exit where I sleep with two pistols I know where to find

And I know how to aim

Because we Astors are inured to hold fast to what we've gained

And we gained the world but not my

Acceptance

And no one reads my fiction . . .

Every dollar

Is a soldier

That will follow

As you're bolder

2. flight 遷徙

Sleeping crammed in a sampan

Only cooled by the breeze of the Nanyang

The workers they need but the workers they hate

With heart under knife we made our escape

Like scattered sand

Or leaves in the wind

Blown far from our land

We're no trouble, we're unseen

3. astor 亞斯德

'Great grandfather tried his luck selling opium to Cathay

But the big conglomerates had sealed that cache

Come war-time with ships under blockade

A stranded Chinese mandarin my great-grandfather offered to convey

So he could send a ship East with his life code

That returned with that pay load

That he invested in land

And the buildings he planned

Where the value soared

As the tenement hordes

Slept packed on the floors

In sub-lease law

No one else would journey North

The work was dirty, it was frozen and cold, and death was on that trail like a constant companion

To make his fortune he ventured forth

From the mud and the pigs that populated the town whose future he foresaw with mansions and slums

He traded hard with the First Nation

Bargained hard for remuneration

The Indians there didn't know business and he plied them with whisky he made himself which he cut with water and spiced with tobacco and harsh red pepper

A gallon cost him 5 cents to make

From the First Nation 50 cents a bottle he would take

It was weak but it dulled their senses

Made them pliant and defenceless

So they would sell for a steal

The profit-making hides of beavers, otters, muskrats and seals

The sea-otter skin he specially sent to the mandarin land

Because even from afar he perceived their demand

900 per cent he would make from fur

So he could lend money to Arron Burr

Because capital discriminates

Between sinners and saints

He lived his life by that simple creed
A dollar was the only soldier he'd need'

4. voyage 迷航

To that extraterritorial treaty port

To work on a ship owned by the foreigners they use to export

I left my village in the Pearl River Delta

Around the Suez Canal at the furnace I swelter

In the bowels of a ship that sails to the West

From our land of the Qing their opium possessed

When they pledged us with gunboats and bargained with muskets

Our decadent bannermen no match for their free trade justice

I work as a trimmer fetching coals from the bunker

Up and down, running with that barrow

The journey to the stoke-hold grows steadily further

As the piles of coal that are nearest are used first for the burner

So your bones they ache and your back it breaks

And you're thirty-five if you're lucky before it takes

The last gasp of your labour

The last snap as it breaks you

Your last breath as it shakes you

Your own death as it takes you

To the land of our ancestors to who we once burned incense

Praying hard as the stick smokes and our reverence is dispensed

Although we toil on the ships of the men from the West

They recruit us in gangs commanded by our fellow black-headed masters

A month's pay he takes, to cover his 'costs'

The Chinese Number One, our god our boss

I had nothing left to bribe him with for the lighter work

So the barrow I run with in the depths and the murk

Where the fumes they choke

And the furnace blasts

Through the thick dark smoke

Of the eighteenth level of hell where I'm cast

Like a superfluous speck of a man from a realm which has strife and warfare and submission and oppression but lacks in grain with earth that won't yield with rivers that burst and break and flood and take but one thing that realm doesn't want for didn't ask for and can't care for is the mighty swell of disposable bodies in a population so so vast

I run all day

I'm beaten if I sway

Or stop

Or drop

Once on shore I'm boarded by another master from my land

And more of my meagre wage they demand

To sleep in crowded quarters of the most menial repose

Where there's barely room to change your clothes

And I can lose more money gambling at fantan

And save even less to take home back to Taishan

But I go to that other place

The quiet space

Where hooded eyes glaze in the gloom

As opiate bliss our cares consume

I pay for the pipe

Inhale and sigh

Lay back on the harsh wooden bench

Sensing my punished bones slowly unclench

As the aches that are part of me sweetly subside

And there

Just a glimpse

Of a smile that's wide

Of a song on the wind

Of a world with no trim

Of mountains and rivers

And lakes of silver

And a woman and a child

. . .

. . .

I won't make it home this time

With money you're a dragon

Without it you're a worm

Find a place that you can build on

And a way to hold on firm . . .

'If your plan is for one year plant rice. If your plan is for ten years plant trees. If your plan is for 100 years educate children'

5. dynasty 王朝

'The founder of our dynasty on the island named by the Munsee Lenape wanted his dollars to be the soldiers that did the bidding of his clan in perpetuity for all time

And why would he not believe that he could accomplish this?

Every single thing he touched turned to gold and his investment thrived

And profit magnified

Through fire and plague and war and the presidents who came and the presidents who went

Whose favour we purchased with the favours we lent

And he designed his will and testament to bequeath half his fortune held in trust

Perhaps we all crave eternity when push comes to shove

But even our founding patriarch

Connot enforce that inheritance ditto mark

If a future generation discovers the audacity

To be fired with philanthropy

Philanthropy

What a quaint word

It's concept blurs

In high walls and paintings and stain-glass shimmer
That bathes me in opulence and balms the stigma'

6. showtime 登台

We jumped ship at the dock in this city sickly with gaslight

We huddled there in the eastern enclave where we made our world and our own kind of street life

We cooked chop suey invented even further West

Where we built railroads and joined the gold quest

They saw us as a peril that was yellow

'The Chinese Must Go' was their angry bellow

They knew our hair was black and our labour was cheap and our need was great and toil was our fate and the earth in our land was made in that shade

But when they coloured us this we knew how far we'd strayed

Here where they write fiction about us

Blame addiction on us

Fear we'll afflict them like us

So they depict us unjust

Three times a week

The bell rings in our Limehouse Chinatown

For a Thomas Cook theme show

Of hatchets and pig-tales and clan wars in silk dressing gowns

We put on a spectacle that belongs on their stage

Turn our street into a zoo and us animals in a cage

While in their theatres they dress up as us

Paint themselves yellow as they perceive us

Tape back their eyes to portray us

In garish imitation that clearly distorts us

7. culture 文化

'It's easy if you're an Astor'

So in the 'West' they call us 'China' and 'Chinese'

I do not even know that means. And I found out later that those words do not exist in the 'Chinese' language

We were the 'Hua Xia' – the 'beautiful grandeur' people – but lots of us were poor so we may have been beautiful but we weren't very grand – we black-headed people who began on the central plains around the Yellow River –

Actually all I know is that my roots are almost definitely in what is now called Southern China which means it's highly debateable whether any trace whatsoever of my ancestral DNA was ever as far North as the central plains around the Yellow River but let's not make a complicated story even more confusing –

– we black-headed people who began on the central plains around the Yellow River – when the tribes of the Huang Di and the tribes of the Yi and the tribes of the Yan Di formed their alliance and became

'The Hundred Surnames'

The Hundred Surnames

That were passed down to

The Ordinary Chinese People who bear witness to history but whose role is presented as small

The Hundred Surnames who eke out a living from arid harsh land

The Ordinary People flung by the sweep of dynastic hand

Faces left blank

Their stories anonymised

Endlessly relentlessly repeatedly colonised

'A good name is better than a good face'

(COUNTER-VOICE, WE HEAR: 'Zhao, Qian, Sun, Li, Zhou, Wu, Zheng, Liang . . . etc.)

'Manhattan

'The island where we all became intoxicated'

And the White man came and the White man cultivated

From muck and brambles came vast buildings and towers and brownstone and pavements and finance and wealth and neon lights and electricity and the theatres of Broadway

And of course the '400 Names'

Of The Gilded Age

In our New York of the New World where we made our stage'

(COUNTER-VOICE, WE HEAR: 'Mr and Mrs F. R. Appleton, Fred H. Allen, Mr and Mrs Astor, Mr and Mrs J. J. Astor . . .)

The Hundred Surnames were passed down to the so-called 'common people' of the Hua Xia – that loose confederation of competing kingdoms that were ruled by warlords that were the size of modern European nations that existed in a state of Total War around the Yellow River

Until they were unified by The First Emperor Qin Shi Huang

The First Emperor

Who burnt the books

And all the intellectuals

He buried them alive

That was our first cultural revolution

And we've gone on and on having cultural revolutions where books are burned and intellectuals are tortured and locked up and killed

Then

After they've died

Rehabilitated

Mountains Above

Blue Skies Behind

'the very rich . . . are different from you and me . . .'

'My aunt The Mrs. Astor created The 400 names of American society

Where you wait four generations

For those ornate relations

And you dance in the ballrooms and soiree with the Stuyvasants and the Whitneys and the Vanderbilts

Where matches are made and the castle is built

On the backs of Irish immigrants who exist in the slums

Where they cough up their lungs

In the biting cold of winter and the searing heat of summer as the sun blazes and burns

While we head uptown and avoid the corners

Head to Newport for the summer
The occasional newcomer
And a yacht on the sea
In that exalted breeze'

8. names 無名氏

'The man who moves a mountain begins by carrying away small stones'

'Wealth does not last beyond three generations'

They kept us Apart

Outside in the Other

They made us all one

Chinese Community

There but not seen

Like ghosts in a dream

We drift and dance and melt in between

Philosopher, tyrant, Arcadian phalansterist, evil genius, victim of narcotics, peddler of narcotics, noble patriot, rabble-rouser, wartime ally, Red Communist threat, frugal peasant, blue ant, seaman, landsman, washerman, laundry-lord, pauper-cook, get-rich-quick-caterer, inscrutable outsider, benighted illiterate, mathematic whiz-kid, likely member of the professions and salatariat, illegal immigrant in the kitchens of Chinatown, illegal immigrant in the back of a lorry, illegal immigrant in the cold grey sea, exploited cockle-picker, apolitical politician, DVD seller, acrobat, background artist, STEM tech worker, golden visa princeling property tycoon, BNO visa job seeker, Burberry clad credit-card consumer shopper, gas-masked street protestor, Instagram activist with subtle Asian traits, content creator, TikTok dancer, aegyo poser, networker, victim of hate crime, community representative wearing national dress in Buckingham Palace queueing up to shake the hand of the monarch of the British Empire, bat eater,

Disease Carrier

But always Apart

And not quite seen

And definitely not heard

Like ghosts in a dream

They made us all one

Chinese Community

9. belonging 歸屬

'I die so many deaths every day

I write stories and builds houses and buy castles and the villa Borghese

My forebear journeyed from Old World to the New

Now I travel back so I can accrue

Holbein portraits and Titian depictions

Of the aristocracy I covet with no restriction

And the Francois Clouet paintings of Edward VI

In this European vista above petty politics

And a small priceless likeness by Louis Cranach

Of Martin Luther in a German throwback

That castle I bought was Anne Boleyn's

Who lost her head for imagined sin

Was there an affinity I felt there to my own fate

In the old new country at the hands of the dread fourth estate?

I'm searching back now through the tree of my family

For any trace of historic aristocracy

Back past the new world where Great Grandfather sent his ship East then headed West following hard

After Lewis and Clark

Back to old Walldorf in the Electoral Palinate

Searching for that ancient blue blood that surely will validate

And make me a Part Of

And no longer Apart

A belonging I crave

That outlasts the grave

And if my offspring don't want it too bad they'll accept it

Like the wealth they inherit

That outwits demerit

When you start out first you use the same fork to eat ice cream and peas

But you assimilate slowly and gradually ease

Into the high life
And the glittering twilight
Welcomes you in
And rewards you with birth right
A fortune that's clasped tight
Until
One comes who tires of the trappings of accumulation
And searches for meaning outside affectation
And riches and hereditary affirmation
In America the Astor legacy is unmade
By The Man Who Gives It All Away
While here my titled Astors preserve our tranche
The English Astors the trunk to the US branch'

10. community 社群

The need to 'unify' the 'Chinese people' is one that often dominates our 'Chinese' imaginary.

Even here in the 'Chinese' diaspora.

Once upon a time in the 'East' we were the 'Hua Xia'. Now here in the 'West' we are the 'Hua Qiao' which is supposed to mean 'overseas Chinese' but it's difficult to translate because the Chinese language is mainly conceptual in its idioms, so that's a 'conceptual expression' for a concrete racial identity which presents as a monolith when we're anything but . . .

Even in Fujian, a relatively small province in what we now call 'China', even in this relatively small province there was historically at least two distinct dialect groups or clans… and they didn't understand each other's languages, they didn't share the same 'culture' and I've been told that at times they didn't even like each other

And that's one relatively small province in a whole vast continent

Which has a dry cereal-producing North and the rice-paddy field dominated South and mountainous regions in the and the seaboards in the East

And then you have Taiwan (controversial) and Hong Kong (controversial) and Singapore (never controversial) and that's without even mentioning – because so often they are not even mentioned - Tibetans and Uyghurs and Hui and Miao and Manchurians and Mongolians – who like the Taiwanese and the Hong Kongese are all supposed to be actually 'Chinese' because they actually live in a 'China' even though they're not actually ethnically 'Chinese' but does the fact that they're not actually ethnically 'Chinese' mean they're more actually 'Chinese' because they actually live in China than us actually ethnically 'Chinese' who don't actually live in 'China'?

All we can definitively say is that we are not all the same

But they like to think we're all the same

And sometimes 'we' like to think we're all the same

And here in Britain

We are the 'Chinese community'

Faces left blank

Stories unseen

Like ghosts in a dream

But now in this Soho Chinatown

All florid gates and gold at sundown

In the cold rain we chant and we march

And a fight breaks out near the Wardour Street arch

That arch that says

This Is Chinese

And We Are Chinese

They made us all one

Chinese Community

But we are Apart

Apart from each other now

Not One Chinese

Every dollar

Is a soldier

That will follow

As you're bolder

With money you're a dragon

Without it you're a worm

Find a place that you can build on

And a way to hold on firm . . .

Find a place that you can cling

And a way to hold on firm . . .

Find some place that you can cling to

that you can cling to

that you can cling to

Find some place

Where you belong

Where they don't hate you
Or hurt you
Or harass you
Or demonise you
Or stigmatise you
Or ostracise you
Or criminalise you
Where you're allowed
Where you're allowed
Where you're not an invader

Where you're not an Outsider
Where you're not a swarm
Where you're not illegal
Where you're not illegal
It's not illegal to be alive
it's not illegal to exist
it's not illegal to resist

it's not illegal to be alive
it's not illegal to exist

T.M.

Ontroerend Goed

Text by Alexander Devriendt, Angelo Tijssens, Aurélie Lannoy, Karolien De Bleser & Samir Veen.

T.M. *is a live, digital, interactive one-to-one experience exploring how media manipulates people, and how conspiracy theories often converge with populist ideologies. The piece is intimate, provocative, and ultimately soulful examination of faith and morality in the contemporary world. In this piece, which is structured like a job interview and thought experiment, an audience member watch video-taped testimonials and interact in real time, in a one-to-one meeting with recruiters (actors) from the 'TM movement.' The object lesson at hand is whether you become part of the club or not, or in so doing, will your soul survive?*

The Belgian theatre-performance-group **Ontroerend Goed** (a punning name, roughly translated as 'Feel Estate') produces self-devised work grounded in the here and now, inviting their audiences to participate as well as observe. The company has made it its trademark to be unpredictable in content and form. Ontroerend Goed delivers intense experiences built in the reality of theatre. Convinced that life goes on during a performance, the group fabricates possible realities that question how we as individuals position ourselves in the world today.

Ontroerend Goed is Alexander Devriendt, Charlotte De Bruyne, Karolien De Bleser, Angelo Tijssens, Aurélie Lannoy, Leonore Spee, Samir Veen, Julia Ghysels, Remi Cosijn, Wim Smet, Beth Thyrion, Jitske Vandenbussche, Hannes Pieters, Luna Boone and Justine Boutens.

The piece premiered online in 2021 as an Ontroerend Goed production in co-production with the Almeida Theatre, ART Happens, Cambridge Junction, Chicago Shakespeare Theater, Esplanade-Theatres on the Bay, Espoon Kaupunginteatteri, Feodor Elutine Impresario Moscow, Festival Internacional de Artes Cenicas Porto Alegre em Cena, Festival Mythos, Kunstencentrum Vooruit, Le Carreau – Scene Nationale de Foix et l'Ariege, Marche Teatro/Inteatro Fetival, Perpodium, RE: LOCATION//by Wildtopia, Richard Jordan Productions, Staatstheater Mainz, Teatro de Barrio Alto, Theatre Royal Plymouth, De Brakke Ground. Directed by Alexander Devriendt.

From the Authors: On *T.M.*

In December 2020 we were once again sitting at home. After a tranquil summer, the virus was on the rise again in Western Europe: shops, theatres and gyms closed, friends and family dinners took place on digital screens. In Belgium, we were allowed to have one 'hugger': one partner, brother, or neighbour we were still allowed to touch. Others would have to wait. The anthropologic theory of social bubbles could barely become more concrete as healthcare rules forced us to select and design social bubbles for ourselves: a small selection of people with whom we could physically interact.

A major part of our lives moved online, the realm where the fringes are at home and where the angriest ones are traditionally the loudest. Right-wing extremism, hateful conspiracy-ideology and fascist enthusiasm seemed rampant. We felt a sense of calamity as we sat on our couches, locked in our bubbles, and watched images of a small group of white supremacists trying to violently overthrow democracy on the other side of the world.

At the same time, the presence of others – especially strangers – also directly endangered our lives through the virus. It was very tempting to conclude we were threatened, and that the threat was in fact other people. That evil and dangerous people, we're very much becoming the norm, rather than the exception.

A year earlier, Rutger Bregman had published his *Humankind: A Hopeful History* (2019), a bestseller trying to convince the reader that humanity is gently natured, that love, compassion, and help are our natural instincts. Bregman argues that the stories of violence and hate are the ones that are echoed and retold, precisely because they are the rare exception, and that we should all strive to fight the idea that our natures, or other peoples, are to be mistrusted. In 2004, when religious terrorism was the publics number one fear, George Saunders published his beautiful PRKA Manifesto in *Slate* magazine.[1] Written in the language of terrorist propaganda, it described the actions of his organization called People Reluctant to Kill for an Abstraction: the declaration of the near entire world population that each minute of each day makes the discission not to kill, rape, bomb, threaten or torture.

From an artistic standpoint, as a lot of theatre's published registrations of their plays online, we had a desire to make a digital work that was both quintessential theatre, while also using the digital online environment as a necessity, rather than just an awkward medium forced by the circumstances.

Those were the original seeds for *T.M.* TM, a show that in some elements returned to our earlier work of one-on-one theatre. T.M., an organization, a weird cult of believers, with a manifesto like George Saunders', vigorously spreading the dogma of human kindness. We designed the show as an introduction course and a one-on-one personality test, with corporate aesthetics and promises like what Scientology uses to lure fresh believers in. Apart from the test, we wanted infomercials of our organization, a manifesto, a way for visitors to meet each other throughout and after the show, and a gift shop selling actual T.M.-merchandise.

Making a digital, online theatre show also provided us with an opportunity to weave the shows premise through its form. Without the physical limitations of classical theatre, we could have people from all over the world in the audience together, at the same time, with a cast of actors from all continents. Connecting visitors from Canada, China and Belgium to actors living in Brazil, Singapore, and Finland. Bringing together different global lives for a moment in time.

The team of *T.M.* started working on the script in the beginning of 2021: scanning questionnaires, applying to Scientology, producing sample questions and meeting daily on Zoom to try them out on each other. At the same time, we started to reach out to partners across the world and started casting actors.

IDFA (International Documentary Filmfestival Amsterdam), one of our partners, connected us to the French design company Upian, who proposed to create an environment that could provide everything we needed on a platform called Ohyay. Ohyay, now discontinued, was a side project from Snapchat developers, who wanted to create an online conference tool that would provide much more options for the user's creativity than the standard 'raster of talking heads' that Zoom, Google Meet or Microsoft Teams provide.

Ontroerend Goed likes to show the system behind a performance, because we think there is a poetic beauty in seeing the cogs and wheels turn that create the theatrical illusion. *T.M.* is the only performance we created where the system behind the experience is a multitude of what the visitor perceives.

T.M. premiered on 21 of April 2021. Every five minutes five new visitors would log in. Twenty theatre venues on four different continents were selling tickets in timeslots. We spread them out in such a way that people would always meet others from different countries when they came to see the show. From the visitor's perspective the show lasts 40 minutes. More than the half of this time is a one-on-one interview: a personality test, with a T.M.- member, one of our actors.

Each day twenty actors would perform for two blocks of three hours each, back-to-back, handling forty visitors an hour for a total of 240 performances a day.

Four operators would be on two copies of the Ohyay-platform, jumping between tabs to connect visitors to actors, keep the system running, provide technical support where needed and play a small one-minute role every few minutes. It was common for visitors to appear without working camera's, microphones, or sound, at which point – keeping with the spirit of the show – an operator would take them to a separate 'room' and try to provide them with technical help to get their hardware working.

We had backstage 'rooms,' where actors could spend time together, share experiences, have a drink. Because the team was spread out over many time zones, some of our actors would be having breakfast, while others were having late night dinners at the same time.

We 'toured' with *T.M.* throughout 2021 and 2022. In November 2021, we recreated a semi-live version for IDFA, where the audience visited a physical T.M.- stand and was welcomed by a receptionist, who would then connect them to an actor online for their intake test. We recreated the original English version in French and Italian. Before 'Ohyay' was discontinued as a platform, we played the show for several thousand people.

Around a one hundred people contributed to *T.M.* in one way or another. Everybody, throughout making, rehearsing, and performing the show, was at home, in their kitchens, living rooms or attics. Many people of the cast have never met each other live, while having spent hundreds of hours together in the performance and our online backstage. There is still an active (private) Facebook-group, where people of our team post pictures when they meet each other for the first time offline. Last month an original T.M.- scarf was spotted by one of our actors on a Parisian subway. We have no idea who the person wearing it was.

Ontroerend Goed

PEOPLE _____ ME

T·M

I AM SO MUCH MORE IN THE 'NOW' NOW

NONE OF US

NO STATUES RAISED FOR ME

SOME OF US

WE DON'T HAVE TO LIKE EACH OTHER. WE MAY NOT. BUT THAT'S FINE. WE DON'T HAVE TO.

RICH PEOPLE SCARE ME.

S. P. B

**ORDINARY.
TYPICAL.
UNREMARKABLE.**

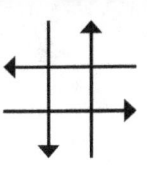

**FEAR
=
DISTRACTION**

MOST OF US   HARDLY EVER MADE THE NEWS   **ALL OF US**

VIL  **GOOD**

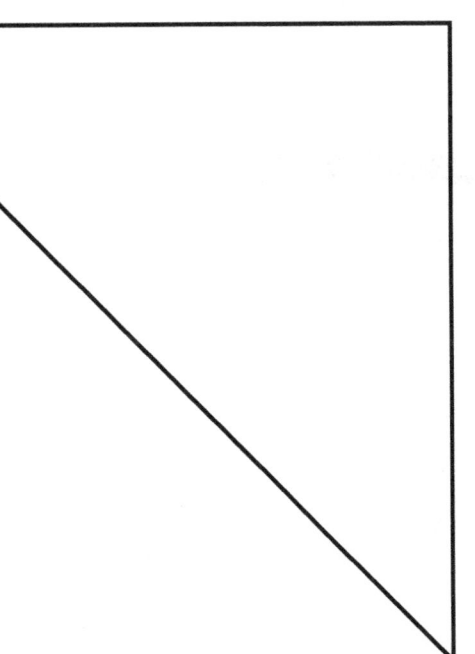

G. O. P.

JOIN US

T·M   RESISTANCE IS FUTILE.

.→ APPROACH

We are many.
We are global.
We are T.M.™
We are a movement.
A worldwide organization.

We were a 2021 performance by Ontroerend Goed.
And now a book, a script, a blueprint for what once was, and one day maybe again will be.

We will challenge you, we will lure you in, we might provoke you, but rest assured: we will guide you, as we have done with thousands before. We will make you hold this book sideways. Because a new perspective will help you see.

This performance, before this book, was online. For one show, dozens of theatres all over the world sold tickets at the same time. If you bought one, you would get an email with an explanation, that would also contain a personal URL. It's the one on the next spread.

In this book, we don't want to just give you a script. We have tried to recreate the same experience by reading this book, that you would have gotten when you saw our show on the screen.

Each fold, 2 pages, you should see as one. The top page will often display an image, this is what you would have seen, full screen.

- → Below the title of a scene is some general scene description on black.
- → Everything on white, is generally spoken text.
  - → *Any description of what is happening is in grey italics, like so.*

If you get confused, it's okay, we all are at different moments in our lives, try to enjoy the ride. You can always flip back to this page. Feel free to put on some music. We suggest anything you like.

We are looking forward to meeting you.
And to welcoming you into the ranks of our still ever-expanding organization.

Resistance is futile.

T·M

CHECKLIST

- **1** ticket = **1** visitor
- use **Google Chrome**
- **doesn't work** on **phones/tablets**
- please wear **headphones**

Dear Visitor,

Thank you very much
for accepting our invitation.

We are looking forward to meeting you.
We are thrilled to introduce you to our organisation.
Thank you for choosing us.
Thank you for choosing T.M.
We hope you will become a part of our
worldwide movement.

01. The **link** below grants you access.
If **google chrome** is not installed on your computer, we advise you to do so.
It will help us make your journey as smooth as possible.
If it is not your default browser, please copy the URL-link into google chrome.
If you are having trouble connecting to us, contact **TM@ontroerendgoed.be**

02. We need to be able to hear and see you.
Make sure your **microphone** and **webcam** are **working**.
We advise wearing **headphones** to avoid any distractions.
And **close** any **other programs** on your computer.
We will require your full attention.

03. T.M. is an **individual experience**.
Please come alone.
And don't be late.

We look forward to our encounter.

Yours,
T.M.

.→ EMAIL INVITATION

After you've bought a ticket through a theatre venue,
you get this email with instructions. It would also
contain a URL, and a specified date and timeslot.

.→ JOIN SECTION

When you go to the link provided in the email,
there is a small login window on a dark blue background.
The URL automatically identifies you as the holder of
the ticket, you type in your name: _____
and press enter.

1 BUFFER ROOM

Your screen changes to a raster of 6 videos. They are all short clips of people around the world, engaging in daily life activities: working, sporting, hanging out. The videos constantly change, they loop separately, so the full image is never the same. Buddies playing basketball at the beach, an elderly woman smiling wholeheartedly over a cup of coffee, a family sharing casual moments. It's like a collage of life around the world. Or more so how television commercials would portray it before showing you the logo of some insurance company. There is no sound to the videos, but an uplifting, slightly airy music plays over your headphones.

↘ After 30 seconds the screen changes to

2 WAITING ROOM

You are in the same 3x2 raster as the room before, but instead of clips there are people there, behind their desks, in front of their laptops or computers.

You see yourself.

Your name is below your image: _____ (your name)

There are 4 other people there: Kim, Chloe, Richard and someone named 'User1234'.

Zoe and Karen are talking to each other. Apparently, they've been here for a few minutes. Richard is having a drink.

The top left image is a TM-logo instead of a person, and the text 'We will be with you shortly' below it. The message changes language every few seconds: English, Spanish, French, Dutch, Chinese, German, Italian, Japanese, back to English.

Suddenly the T.M.-Logo changes and a person wearing a grey polo with a T.M.-logo on it appears. He is wearing a headset and is in front of a grey backdrop. His name is below his image too: Mario (T.M. Belgium). He seems to be an operator, a sort of receptionist of this system.

Mario T.M. BELGIUM

Good afternoon, everybody,
It's a pleasure to meet you.
Are you all able to hear and see me?

People nod

Let me check your microphone.
Kim, in what country are you now?

Kim Germany

Thank you. User1234, how about you?

User1234 I'm in Belgium

User1234, people will use the name you've chosen throughout the performance to address you. If you want to change it to something else, you can now still do so in settings. It's the icon of the cogwheel on top of your screen.

The operator is silent for 30 seconds or so as he seems to be doing something technical.

Thank you.

Let's also set our browser to full screen mode so we can have your full attention. For mac users press the control button, the command button and the F button at the same time. For the mac users that still see their toolbar, now also press shift command and F at the same time. If you are on Windows, please press the F11 button, it's one button on the top of your keyboard. You should be full screen right now. Did we all do that successfully?

People nod.

It's a pleasure to meet you, Kevin.

Kevin Thank you, done!

Chloe?

Chloe I'm in Hong Kong

Ah, good... evening then, in your case?

Yes! Good evening.

Richard?

Richard the U.K.

Richard *laughs as he remarks:*
I never knew you could do that!

Well, we learn every day.

And finally, _____ (your name)? **(your name)** I'm in _____

Thank you. Could you all please take a moment to turn off your phone. Close all other programs and silence any distractions.

I would like to start you off with a short introduction of our organisation.

I wish you all a pleasant journey.

3 INTRODUCTION ROOM

You see a woman wearing the same headset, polo with T.M.-logo, and in front of a similar backdrop as the operator you just met. She's looking directly at you. It's not staring, she seems to be inspecting, looking, measuring you. Is this live? Or a video? There does not seem to be any response when you say 'hi'.

```
It takes 20 or so seconds before she starts talking:
```

So, now that I have your attention: Welcome to T.M.
And thank you, for being here, for listening. That is exactly what we appreciate in you. You are here to experience something. You are looking for something that questions what you know, questions what you believe in.

You want to challenge your own worldview. Well, you came to the right place. That is exactly what T.M. can give you.
That is our organisation. You might think that we are new, because you never heard of us. But we have always been here. We are as old as humanity. We made history.
Today you will get to know us, and we will get to know you.
Once you know who we are there is no turning back
you will see us everywhere: on the street, the bus, in your house, but most of all: every time you look in the mirror, you'll see T.M.
And now you probably wonder: what is T.M.?
T.M. is wisdom. T.M. is knowledge. T.M. is an organisation of truth. It's a way to understand the world, understand ourselves in a better way. What we preach is based on 10.000 years of experience. We're honoured and lucky to be a small part of this worldwide organisation.

different testimonial videos, see discription

/ CUT TO / A man in his 30's with a welcoming smile, carrying study books:

At first, I thought, these people were just trying to sell me something – that's a natural reflex: we think others are out the profit off of us, but I listened and learned that that was not the case: yes, there is profit, a lot of profit to be made, but it's all mine. I'm richer now as I have access to the wealth of ideas T.M. has to offer.

/ CUT TO / A man is his late 20's, behind the wheel of his car in a parking lot, a McDonalds vaguely in the background:

I learned a lot, really. It takes some time, like all difficult things. But now I can honestly say, my life will never be the same again. I'm so proud of myself.

/ CUT TO / A man in an apron in the kitchen of a restaurant:

Before T.M., fear used to control me. Now I realise, it's just a distraction. I'm so much more in the 'now' now.

/ CUT TO / A woman in her 50's, well dressed in a spacious home office:

For me, it was like I had been looking all along, but I wasn't really seeing, like I never noticed there was a filter between me and the rest of the world. But only now that it's gone, I realise how clouded my view was.

/ CUT TO / A woman early 20's, speaking Cantonese in a busy Asian city, subtitled:

I have two science degrees, but what T.M taught me, I could never have imagined...

/ CUT TO / Same woman in home office:

All it took for me to get where I am now, is to actually start the journey.

/ CUT TO / Same man in car:

Welcome.

/ CUT TO / Same man in apron, in an African language, subtitled:

Welcome.

/ CUT TO / Same man carrying studying books:

Welcome. Glad to see you.

/ CUT TO / Same T.M.-woman in front of grey backdrop:

You already took the first step. You are here. That is the first step in becoming a member. At this very moment, one of our colleagues is dying to meet you. They will ask you a series of questions. A test. A test that will determine if you can become a part of T.M.: if you can become an ambassador for humanity. Don't worry. We are here to guide you. We're sure you'll manage. Because we believe in you. Hey, after all, why shouldn't we?

4 INTERVIEW

Another woman, full screen.
Wearing the same outfit, headset,
same backdrop as the ones before.
She is looking at you. Not
staring, inspecting, measuring,
curiously.

... What follows is an interview,
a questionnaire or quiz of some
sort, with personal questions
aimed at forming a psychological
profile of you. There is room to
answer each question, to think,
to elaborate on your answers.
Sometimes the interviewer will
ask follow-up questions or ask
you to specify. During this she
makes notes. For the purpose of
experience, we have listed
only questions here, without
sample answers, or follow-ups that
would naturally flow from your
answers, which would create a more
interactive, personal, experience
than we portray in this book
version.

Now that I have your attention.

She takes a pen

Hi _____ (your name).
Welcome.
My name is Rafaela from T.M. Brazil
Do you like answering questions?

		Y	N
Rafaela T.M. BRASIL			
	Do you like yes or no questions?	○	○
	Are you going to try to answer my questions honestly?	○	○
	Have you ever killed someone?	○	○
	Would you like to know how it feels to die?	○	○
	Would you rather be able to see your own future or the future of humanity?	○	○
	Do you think the world could be a better place?	○	○
	Do you deserve to be richer than you are?	○	○
	Do rich people scare you?	○	○
	Do poor people scare you?	○	○
	Are humans dangerous?	○	○
	Are you dangerous?	○	○
	Have you ever witnessed a murder in person?	○	○
	And fictional murders: how many fictional murders would you estimate you saw in the past month?		
	Now, I could show you a video that shows a real murder. Would you like to see it?	○	○
	Okay. I'll make a note of that.		
↘ She marks something and moves on without showing you the video.			
	Are you afraid of pure evil?	○	○
	Does pure evil exist?	○	○
	Have you ever experienced pure evil yourself?	○	○
	Do you think that most people would answer _____ (your last answer)?	○	○

In a moment, I will read you a few short statements.
You let me know if you believe the statement is true for:

none of us / some of us / most of us / all of us.

↘ On an overlay 4
options appear at the
bottom of the screen.

Here we go:

I am hungry — none of us / some of us / most of us / all of us.

I am poor — none of us / some of us / most of us / all of us.

I am lonely — none of us / some of us / most of us / all of us.

I am racist — none of us / some of us / most of us / all of us.

I do things for money — none of us / some of us / most of us / all of us.

I am a good person — none of us / some of us / most of us / all of us.

Are you a good person _____ (your name)?

I will now read you some words and you have to reply with the first word that comes to your mind. Don't overthink it, just answer as quickly as possible.

scissors	
people	
five	
children	
airplane	
money	
fear	
city	
circle	

Are you a member of a terrorist organisation?

For the next question, we will use a scale of 1 to 20.
1 being pure evil and on the other side of the scale: 20, perfectly good.

↘ On the screen 1 appears on the bottom left, and 20 on the bottom right

Where would you place yourself _____ (your name)?	... / 20
Where would you place yourself on that scale 10 years ago?	... / 20
Where would you place yourself as a teenager?	... / 20
And as a newborn child?	... / 20
Are all babies a _____ (last answer)?	
Can a baby be a bad person?	
Can a 7 year old be a bad person?	
Can a 14 year old be a bad person?	
How old are you, _____ (your name)?	

Now, let's go back to our scale of 1 to 20.

What about most people you know: your friends, family, where would you place them on average?	... / 20
And the average of people you don't know?	... / 20
And nurses, where would they be on the scale?	... / 20
And CEOs?	... / 20
CEOs of big oil companies?	... / 20
And your parents, where would you place your mother?	... / 20
And your father?	... / 20
Just to make sure, 17, 18, 19 are still not taken. Could you ever be a 19?	
Are good people always nice people?	
If possible: so in your life you went from a ... / 20, as a baby, to a ... / 20, which you are now. What happened that made you go down?	
If all people would be like you, would the world be a better place?	

↘ *Experience learns that most people rarely quote 17, 18, 19.*

Could you complete this sentence for me?
Answer what feels the most true for you: a, b, c, d or e?

people

me

a. love
b. scare
c. surprise
d. don't notice
e. shouldn't leave

_____ (your name), let's imagine you just won the lottery.
Congratulations!
What will you do with the money?

Do you play the lottery?

↘ on screen a text
overlay appears:
people _____ me

↘ She repeats part of
your answer out loud.
it seems to be the part
where you spend the money
on others.

Okay _____ (your name)
I'm going to ask you to close your eyes.

Now imagine yourself sitting right here, in your room.

Everything is there: furniture, objects.

But gradually, an intense light starts to fill the space.

It becomes so bright that everything around you seems to disappear.

You can't distinguish between wall or floor or ceiling.
Everything is flooded with light.

You are looking at your hands, but you can barely see them.
It is no longer clear where you end and where the room begins.

E v e r y t h i n g   i s   l i g h t .

Now consider if you have any particular feeling right now.
Analytical psychologists say this is how you feel about dying.

You can open your eyes.

Are you carrying any weapons?

Is there an object nearby that could be used to kill someone?

Any sharp objects, any heavy objects?

Now, imagine yourself killing me with that object. Say "yes" when I'm dead.

Okay go.

↘ *She is sitting still and looking directly at the camera, while you imagine what it would look like to kill her with the weapon you picked.*

● T.M. *We kept track of the weapon and time that was used to kill the actor in every show. Creating an ever expanding list of ways we died. Here's an excerpt:*

chair (0'02")
lamp (0'04")
plantpot (0'06")
cable (0'19")
heavy book (0'07")
paperweight (0'25")
knife (0'02")
mango (3'44")
shoelace (0'41")
bare hands (0'04")
Peppa Pig puzzle (0'07")

speaker (0'08")
metal spoon (0'20")
deodorant (0'16")
pencil (0'18")
papercutter (1'02")
kitchen knife (0'06")
extension cord (0'13")
pillow (0'34")
wooden box (0'08")
desk thingy for pencils (0'08")
usb cable (0'41")
belt (0'19")
monitor (0'06")
shoe (0'11")
picture frame (0'18")
wooden stick (0'05")
hands (0'09")
walking cane (1'07")
crème-brulee flamer (0'43")
sword (0'11")
water bucket (1'00")
pidgeon cage (0'07")
hand (0'04")
airfryer (0'19")
chopsticks (in eye) (0'03")
pencil (1'11")
gun (0'01")
cable (0'22")
t-shirt (0'11")
kitchen knife (0'07")
extension cord (0'18")
tea pot (0'03")
bat (0'15")
basketball (in face) (0'08")
pan (0'07")
bottle (0'16")
2 forks (0'21")
cable (0'09")
baby crib (0'08")
nunchuks (0'03")
plate (0'09")
wine bottle (0'04")
patato knife (0'06")

iPad (0'19")
cable (0'53")
tennis racket (0'08")
stick (0'11")
thrown from window (0'03")
monitor (0'08")
cheese cutter (0'04")
coffee pot (0'02")
cable (0'21")
knife (0'03")
fork (0'01")
hands (0'50")
airsoft gun (0'04")
rope (1'32")
blue BIC (0'28")
3 cables bound togheter (0'06")
darts (0'08")
keychain (0'16")
drowned in bathtub (0'11")
cucumber (0'39")
hockey stick (0'05")
dustbin (0'03")
crossbow (0'02")
toothpicks (1'08")
piece of string (0'19")
painting (0'08")
matches (0'23")
USB-C cable (0'28")
fist (1'09")
wig (0'19")
knife (0'11")
baseball glove (0'22")
hot oil (0'29")
family bust (0'02")
tablet (0'04")
tennis racket (0'09")
steak knife (0'04")
frozen fish (0'22")
cable (0'12")
DVD box (0'16")
mouse-cord (0'09")
plate (0'05")
paper cuts (0'23")
CD-ROM (0'07")

rat poison (0'22")
fists (punching) (0'08")
plate (0'18")
pen (0'05")
pen (1'01")
piece of metal (0'18")
french press (0'09")
dunbell (0'02")
table (0'02")
wooden plate (0'13")
really sharp pencil (0'07")
windowpane (0'02")
knife (0'08")
keys (0'41")
blower (0'04")
painting (0'06")
hockey stick (0'22")
tv tray (0'07")
cellphone (0'08")
cable (0'08")
bow (for sports) (0'01")
bic (0'04")
tea pot (0'07")
coffee mug (0'54")
comp mouse (0'12")
rocking chair (0'09")
kite (0'20")
part of wooden fence (0'06")
föhn (1'27")
pencil (0'22")
statue (0'03")
bubble wrap (0'30")
an Andy Warhol reproduction (0'43")
sword (0'03")
tray from freezer (0'12")
plastic pony (0'02")
knife (0'08")
paperclips (0'38")
coaster (0'04")
beer bottle (0'29")

Am I dead?

Yes

Okay, thank you.

_____ (your name), before we proceed, we will watch a short video:

↘ / CUT TO / a short video (around a minute and a half). It's a slightly edited version of the 1944 'Heider and Simmel simulation'. Three shapes: a small triangle, a larger triangle and a small circle move around the screen. It's animated in such a way, that it's easy to project a simple story on the shapes. To describe them as characters. Where the larger shape is bullying the smaller ones. In the end, the smaller shapes outwit their bully and get away safely. The point of the video, and the original research, is that the human mind instinctively creates stories, and has no problem projecting feelings on it, even if the characters are as abstract as a triangle or a circle.

 _____ / YOU CAN WATCH THE ORIGINAL VIDEO HERE /

Can you describe what you saw?
_____

Where would you put the big triangle on our scale from 1 to 20? 1 being pure evil, 20 perfectly good.
_____

The numbers 1 and 20 appear on the screen again.
_____

And the small circle?
_____

The small triangle?
_____

Do you base your opinion more on emotions or on facts?
_____

↘ She nods. She starts to gather some papers. ticks some things off.

↘ She gathers some papers, writes a few things down, seems to do some short calculations, before she looks up, and gives you your evaluation. Part of the sentences and conclusions are scripted, others depend on the answers you've given throughout the show. Here, we have put down an example monologue of how a typical show would end:

Do you want to know how well you performed on this test?

On a scale from 1 to 20, 1 being pure evil and 20 perfectly good, you are an 18. You're not a 12.
According to you, making decisions for your benefit instead of others made you a 12, we disagree.

Your answers reflect that your principles are based on honesty, justice & helping others. You were the first one to associate the word children with talent.

Questions where you had to pass judgement on other people took you longer than questions where you had to judge yourself.

The question that took you the longest was 'was when you had to place your mother on a scale from 1 to 20'
It took you 13 seconds to kill me.
The average is 9 seconds.
You used a kitchen knife.
Other objects used were pens & computer cables,
And once I got killed with a Peppa Pig puzzle.
You base your opinions more on emotions than on facts, you are manipulable, but you seem to be aware of it.
And people surprise you.

Congratulations, you made it.
You are a member of T.M.,
you are part of The Majority, a Small Part of a Big Group of Ordinary People

And this is our manifesto:

↘ / CUT TO / A man, once again in the same outfit and backdrop. He starts talking as soon as he appears on the screen.

↘ Numbers from 1 to 11 appear on the screen while he sums up the T.M.-manifesto.

We hold the following to be true:

1. On a scale from one to twenty: We are all good people, we are better than we think we are.

2. We do not kill, we are reluctant to commit evil.

3. We can imagine being dangerous, we know what violence looks like. But we choose not to use violence as an option.

4. Fearing other members is a waste of time. It distracts us.

5. We know that evil is strong, loud and exceptional. We know that good is ordinary, typical, the usual.

6. We are aware that we base our opinion more on emotions than on facts. We are manipulable, but in the end, we try to return to reason.

7. We are masters of imagination, we create the most beautiful and the most horrible stories. That is our weakness and our strength.

8. The possibility that we are wrong about you, that you are not a member, is smaller than winning the lottery.

9. We don't have to like each other. We may not. But that's fine. We don't have to.

10. We all worry if these statements are true. We don't always dare to believe them. We have doubts.

11. We care for each other. We even care for small triangles. We all try to make the world a better place.

This is what we believe.
This is us.
We are T.M.
We are The Majority.
We are many.

↘ / CUT TO / a 3x2 raster, like the ones you've seen earlier. The man talking is on one of the spaces. You are in one. You also see Kim and Chloe. 2 of other visitors you've met at the beginning, and some people you haven't seen.

We are worldwide.
We are born, we fall in love. Sometimes we wake up in the middle of the night, wondering if we made the right decision. We have hopes, we are hopeless. We vote left, we vote right. In moments of crisis, we pat one another awkwardly on the back, mumbling shy truisms.

↘ / CUT TO / a 2x3 raster. 6 people. You see yourself. all the others you've met at the beginning.

We hardly ever make the news, the history books.
We are a big group of ordinary people. There are people who oppose us. They are loud and steal the attention. They create a momentary ripple on the water of life. But what they do is an exception. We are many.
We, in fact, outnumber them. We are more.

↘ / CUT TO / Bigger raster. Even more people. 12 or so. You can find yourself. and the man talking.

We are The Majority. People love us, people scare us, people don't notice us, sometimes people surprise us. People should never leave us. Because the more we are, the more we can achieve.

↘ / CUT TO / 25 people or so. Somewhere among all those faces is you. You recognise others.

↘ / CUT TO / 50 or more people.

↘ / CUT TO / Even more people. a hundred or more.

Join us

Resistance is futile

↘ / CUT TO / Many, many more people. Hundreds. People. looking. nodding. listening. talking. People smiling. looking sceptic. angry. weird. normal. boring. interesting. happy. lonely. Hundreds of different lives. Some only just beginning. some almost at an end. each at the centre of its own walk. An unfathomable richness of emotions. passions. sadness. desires. anger. fascinations. love. You must be there. somewhere between all those faces. but you can't find yourself. you have blended in. becoming anonymous. Hundreds different paths. diverging. meeting each other in this one moment. these few seconds. before they are all gone. back down their own road.

5 DECOMPRESSION ROOM

A grey backdrop, with a menu of buttons. Small circles appear with the people in it you've met at the beginning: Kim, Richard, Kevin, Chloe and you. There are also some people there you haven't seen before. You can talk to them, ask how their experience was. What they are thinking. Ask what number they scored in their tests. When you press one of buttons you get an overlay, you keep seeing and hearing the others.

You can:
[Read Manifesto], with the 11 declarations of T.M.
As you just heard.

Enter a [Gift Shop] where you can buy T.M.-merchandise: a coffee mug, a shawl, pens, pencils, blanket. They contain phrases and declarations of the show. And are in grey/orange T.M. design. Profits go to amnesty International.

View the [credits]. The list of actors is over 50 names long. You see English, Dutch, Chinese, Spanish, Portuguese names, very different. The list of coproducers is very long, and they seem to be all over the world.

[Leave a message] on the message board. There is a long list of messages from others that saw the same show. When you look at the dates, all messages are from today. Dozens of shows must be going on at the same time.

T.M

READ THE MANIFESTO

LEAVE US A MESSAGE

EVIL ⟵——⟶ GOOD

S.P.B.G.O.P.

JOIN US

VISIT THE GIFTSHOP

WATCH THE CREDITS

T.M CREDITS

director
Alexander Devriendt

text
Alexander Devriendt
Angelo Tijssens
Aurélie Lannoy
Karolien De Bleser
Samir Veen

scenography/design/costumes
David Williamson
Nick Mattan

video
David Williamson
Angelo Tijssens

sound
Senjan Jansen

cast
Aaron J. Gordon
Adina Macpherson
Alexander Sinyakovich
Alexey Lyubimov
Ana Vilela da Costa
André Varela
Angelo Tijssens
Aurélie Lannoy
Cedric Coomans
Charlotte De Bruyne
Crispian Chan
Crista Alfaiate
Daniel Mutlu
Daria Bashkirova
Ekaterina Shibaeva
Ellison Tan Yuyang
Emilie Bisetti
Florian Pautasso
Francesca Gabucci
Gabriela Poester
Giacomo Lilliù
Hendrik Kegels
João Abreu
Johannes Wirix-Speetjens
Julia Ghysels
Karolien De Bleser
Leonore Spee
Lisa Schamlé
Louise Pascal
Luca Bryssinck
Luca Persan
Marjan De Schutter
Marieke Anthoni
Marie Peeters
Flora Ramakers
Robin Keyaert
Samir Veen
Sascha Bornkamp
Sonja Van Oijen
Tiffer Hutchings
Tijmen Govaerts
Vincent Doddema
Goua Robert Grovogui
Ikram Aloued
Ingeborg Sergeant
Jeroen Van der Ven
Mathis Schellekens
Sachli Gholamalizad
Zach Hatch
Zoe Chan

software
created by Upian in Ohyay
Adélaïde Desnoë
Gregory Trowbridge
Sébastien Brothier

technical support
Pepijn Mesure
Sarah Feyen

production planning
Charlotte Nyota Bischop
David Bauwens
Marie Peeters

special adviser
Caspar Sonnen
Toby Coffey

special thanks to
Zwart op Wit

production
Ontroerend Goed

co-production
Almeida Theatre (UK)
Art Happens (BE)
Cambridge Junction (UK)
Chicago Shakespeare Theater (US)
Esplanade – Theatres on the Bay (SG)
Espoon Kaupunginteatteri (FI)
Feodor Elutine Impresario Moscow (RU)
Festival Internacional de Artes
Cênicas Porto Alegre em Cena (BR)
Festival Mythos (FR)
Kunstencentrum Vooruit (BE)
Le Carreau - Scène Nationale de
Forbach et de l'Est mosellan (FR)
L'ESTIVE Scène Nationale de Foix et l'Ariège (FR)
Marche Teatro/Inteatro Festival (IT)
Perpodium (BE)
RE:LOCATION// by Wildtopia (DK)
Richard Jordan Productions (UK)
Staatstheater Mainz (DE)
Teatro do Bairro Alto (PT)
Theatre Royal Plymouth (UK)
Vlaams Cultuurhuis de Brakke Grond (NL)

co-commissioned by
IDFA DocLab (NL)
National Theatre
Immersive Storytelling Studio (UK)

with the support of
the Flemish Government
and the City of Ghent.
This show was made possible
with the support of the Tax
Shelter measure from the
Belgian Federal Government
via Cronos Invest

book version
Samir Veen
Remi Cosijn
Nick Mattan

Note on the Editor

Caridad Svich is a 2024 Guggenheim Foundation Fellow. Her plays and translations have been produced across the US and abroad. Of Cuban-Argentine-Spanish-Croatian descent, her work centres on environmental and human rights, examines the poetics and politics of resistance, neoliberalism and its effects on culture and society, and often radically reconfigures the classics through the aesthetics of transmedia theatre. Key pieces include *12 Ophelias*, *Iphigenia Crash Land Falls . . .*, *Red Bike* and *The House of the Spirits* (based on Isabel Allende's novel). Among her honours are: Flora Roberts Award (The Dramatists Guild), Obie for Lifetime Achievement, Ellen Stewart Career Achievement Award (ATHE), American Theatre Critics Association Primus Prize, Edgerton Foundation New Play Award and a Harvard/Radcliffe Institute Fellowship. She has authored/edited several books including *Toward a Future Theatre* (Methuen Drama), *Audience Revolution* and *Federico Garcia Lorca: Impossible Theatre*. She is also published by TRW Plays, Broadway Play Publishing, Intellect Books, and more. As a screenwriter, the feature film *Fugitive Dreams* is streaming on Apple TV and Amazon Prime. They are founder of NoPassport theatre alliance and press, Co-Artistic Director at the Lucille Lortel Theater, Drama Editor at *Asymptote* literary journal, and an editor at *Contemporary Theatre Review*. She teaches playwriting and creative writing at Rutgers University-New Brunswick, NYU School of Professional Studies and Tisch, and the Einhorn School of Performing Arts at Primary Stages Theatre. website: https://caridadsvich.com

Selected Bibliography

Aebischer, Pascale. *Viral Shakespeare: Performance in the Time of the Pandemic* (Cambridge: Cambridge University Press, 2021).
Allred, G. K., Broadribb, B. (ed.) and Sullivan, E. (ed.). *Lockdown Shakespeare: New Evolutions in Performance and Adaptation* (London: Bloomsbury Drama, 2022).
Auslander, Philip. *Performance in a Mediatized Culture*, third edition (London and New York: Routledge, 2023).
Bauman, Zygmunt. *Liquid Modernity* (Cambridge, MA: Polity Press, 2000).
Bauman, Zygmunt. *Retrotopia* (Cambridge, MA: Polity Press, 2017).
Bay-Cheng, Sarah, Parker-Starbuck, Jennifer and Saltz, David Z. *Performance and Media: Taxonomies for a Changing Field* (Ann Arbor: University of Michigan Press, 2015).
Blake, Bill. *Theatre & the Digital* (London: Red Globe Press, 2014).
Brown, Kevin. *Karaoke Idols: Popular Music and the Performance of Identity* (Bristol: Intellect Books, 2015).
Causey, Matthew. *Theatre and Performance in Digital Culture: from simulation to embeddedness* (London and New York: Routledge, 2006).
Chemers, Mark and Sell, Mike. *Systemic Dramaturgy: A Handbook for the Digital Age* (Carbondale, IL: Southern Illinois University, 2022).
Cortazar, Julio. Trans. Gregory Rabassa. *Hopscotch* (NY: Pantheon, 1966, English language edition).
Davis, Mike, *The Monster Enters: COVID-19, Avian Flu, and the Plagues of Capitalism* (London and Brooklyn: Verso Books, 2020).
Dimitrova, Zornitsa. *Theatre and the Virtual: Genesis, Touch, Gesture* (London and New York: Routledge, 2024).
Dixon, Steve. *Digital Performance: A History of New Media* (Cambridge: MIT Press, 2007).
Dundjerovic, Aleksandar Sasha. *Live Digital Theatre: Interdisciplinary Performance Pedagogies* (London and New York: Routledge, 2023).
Fisher, Mark. *Ghosts of My Life: Writings on Depression, Hauntology, Lost Futures* (Winchester, UK: Zero Books, 2022).
Giannachi, Gabriella. *Virtual Theatres: An Introduction* (Oxfordshire: Taylor & Francis, 2004).
Giannachi, Gabriella, Nick Kaye and Michael Shanks. *Archaeologies of Presence: Art, Performance and the Persistence of Being* (Abingdon and New York: Routledge, 2012).
Joyce, Michael. *afternoon, a story* (Watertown, MA: Eastgate Systems, 1987–91).
Kinder, Marsha and McPherson, Tara (eds). *Transmedia Frictions: The Digital, the Arts and the Humanities* (Oakland, CA: University of California Press, 2014).
Masura, Nadja. *Digital Theatre: The Making and Meaning of Live Mediated Performance, US & UK 1990–2020.* (London: Palgrave Macmillan, 2020).
Moore, Jason W. *Anthropocene or Capitalocene? Nature, History, and the Crisis of Capitalism* (Oakland: PM Press, 2016).
Myles, Robert, and Clayman Pye, Valerie. *Innovation & Digital Theatremaking: Rethinking Theatre with 'The Show Must Go Online'* (London and New York: Routledge, 2023).
Oliszewski, Alex, Fine, Daniel, and Roth, Daniel. *Digital Media, Projection Design, and Technology for Theatre* (London and New York: Routledge, 2018).
Radosavljevic, Duska. *Aural/Oral Dramaturgies* (London and New York: Routledge, 2023).
Read, Alan. *Theatre in the Expanded Field* (London: Bloomsbury, 2013).
Russell, Legacy Russell. *Glitch Feminism* (London and Brooklyn: Verso Books, 2020).
Salter, Chris. *Entangled: Technology and the Transformation of Performance* (Cambridge, MA: MIT Press, 2010).

Sullivan, Erin. *Shakespeare and Digital Performance in Practice* (Palgrave Macmillan, 2022).
Virilio, Paul with Bertrand Richard, translated by Ames Hodges. *The Administration of Fear* (Cambridge, MA: Semiotext (e), 2012).
Zuboff, Shoshana. *The Age of Surveillance Capitalism* (New York: Public Affairs, Hachette Book Group, 2018).